Science and the Bible
Evidence-Based Christian Belief

SCIENCE
AND THE BIBLE

EVIDENCE-BASED
CHRISTIAN BELIEF

Ted Burge

TEMPLETON *T* FOUNDATION PRESS
PHILADELPHIA AND LONDON

Templeton Foundation Press
300 Conshohocken State Road, Suite 550
West Conshohocken, PA 19428
www.templetonpress.org

Templeton Foundation Press helps intellectual leaders and others learn about science research on aspects of realities, invisible and intangible. Spiritual realities include unlimited love, accelerating creativity, worship, and the benefits of purpose in persons and in the cosmos.

The first version of chapter 10 appeared in *The Gloucester Compass* with the title "Today's Story of Creation-5th June 1998." The article was also published in *The Church Times*, November 28, 1998; in *God for the 21st Century*, edited by Russell Stannard (Templeton Foundation Press, 2000); and in *Thinking Through Religion, Teacher's Resource File* (Oxford University Press, 2000).

Library of Congress Cataloging-in-Publication Data

Burge, Ted.
  Science and the Bible : evidence-based Christian belief / Ted Burge.
    p. cm.
  Includes bibliographical references and index.
  ISBN 1-932031-93-6 (alk. paper)
  1. Bible and science. 2. Apologetics. I. Title.
  BS650.B79 2005
  261.5'5—dc22

                               2005008232

ISBN 13: 978-1-932031-93-5
ISBN 10: 1-932031-93-6

Designed and typeset by Gopa & Ted2, Inc. in Requiem
Printed in the United States of America

05 06 07 08 09 10   10 9 8 7 6 5 4 3 2 1

Jesus said,
God is Spirit
and those who worship him
must worship in Spirit
and Truth.
—JOHN 4:24

I still have many things to say to you,
but you cannot bear them now.
When the Spirit of truth comes,
he will guide you into all the truth.
—JOHN 16:12–13

And the truth will make you free.
—JOHN 8:32

Contents

Foreword

ELIGIOUS BELIEF may go beyond what can be inferred from the evidence of the world about us, but it must never ignore that evidence. A faith which rides roughshod over what reason and observation tell us of our situation not only can never in the end hope to commend itself to more than a minority, but will also cut that minority off from the bulk of humankind and distort the souls and corrupt the integrity of those who hold it.

Over the last 300 years our knowledge of the universe and ourselves has grown with exponential speed and, in the view of many, has left religious and, specifically, Christian belief far behind. But a good number of those well qualified to judge are convinced that the core beliefs of Christian faith are still of crucial importance for human well-being and do not in fact conflict with our new knowledge. Faith can stand firm on the evidence.

Among those especially well equipped to present this fresh account of Christian belief, Ted Burge occupies a distinguished place. As an emeritus professor of physics in London University he has unchallengeable scientific credentials. But as a committed layman of the Church of England, whose books of private and public devotion, *Lord of All*, *Hear Our Prayer*, and *Lord for All Seasons*, are widely valued for combining spirituality and realism, he has become known also as someone of authentic contemporary faith.

In *Science and the Bible: Evidence-Based Christian Belief* we have the latest prayerful fruit of the interaction between his scientific and theological study and reflection, and we can only be deeply grateful for what will, I am sure, prove for many a stimulating and timely resource.

The Right Reverend John Austin Baker, M.A., M.Litt., D.D.

Preface

THE TITLE OF THIS BOOK raises the question "On what do people base their Christian beliefs?" Many Christians would answer without any hesitation, "On the Bible, of course," and they would include a wide range of emphases and interpretations. Others would reply, "The teachings of the Church," and again there would be a variety of churches, denominations, and traditions. Yet others, when pressed, would want to say they are based on their personal experience, with a whole spectrum of contributions—individual spiritual experience, influences in the home, in a church, and in schools and universities, experience of other religions, and experience stemming from their knowledge of the Bible, science, history, and the arts.

As a member of University staff, in the course of my research, I had been deeply interested in the obtaining of evidence in a particular field, nuclear physics, and how to evaluate it. As a Christian with a robust interest in theology, and particularly its relation to science, it seemed to me that I simply had to study the evidence for and against my beliefs. This book is the result, and its obvious limitations in treating such an enormous subject are an open invitation to fellow believers, or disbelievers, to continue the study, or criticize this contribution. It is expected to be of interest to those who value their religious beliefs, or lack of them, and feel that they need to be supported by deeper study both of religious evidence and related scientific and other discoveries and beliefs.

We need to examine what we accept as evidence for our religious beliefs, and also what we see as evidence for our scientific beliefs. Generally speaking, our scientific beliefs are based on the authoritative statements of respected scientists. Evidence for religious beliefs has a wider range of qualities than evidence from science. Individual religious experience cannot be the same for everybody, and interpretation of evidence is a deep problem, especially when the evidence is found in the text of the Bible.

The results of science that are relevant to religious beliefs are unlikely to be influential if science itself is not respected. Some people seem to have an inbuilt fear and distrust of science, and much of this is because they do not have sufficient knowledge of the methods of science. Distrust of science is sometimes based on misapplications of technology rather than on fundamental knowledge of the Universe, which is the proper realm of science. For me, knowledge of science is knowledge of God's creation and often helps to identify some of the things we can say about God.

Acknowledgments

My TITLE was suggested by a seminal volume, *Evidence-Based General Practice,* by Dr. Leone Ridsdale, a sometime colleague of my wife. Published in 1995, the book reflected the interests of the *Evidence-Based Medicine Working Group* (1992), based in Ontario, Canada. This approach to medicine continues to excite interest and command respect.

Several friends have read this present book, or parts of it, at various stages in its development. In particular, I thank Bishop John Baker for his detailed and perceptive comments and for providing the foreword, Professor Owen Gingerich, Professor Bill Hull, and the Reverend John F. Foster, S.J., for their commendations. Helpful comments were made by Professor Roy Niblett, the Reverend John Green, and friends in Painswick—retired teacher of religious education Judith O'Riordan, retired teacher and Roman Catholic Kate Davie, former missionary and retired social worker Alison Robinson, retired chartered accountant Hywel James, and Elizabeth Finsberg. Bill Varah recommended the books by Rohl and by Phillips on the new chronology for archaeology.

The editorial assistance of Templeton Foundation Press has been much appreciated. The final text is my own choice, and no blame for errors or infelicities attaches to any of those who made comments.

Some of the material has already been published elsewhere, as acknowledged in the text.

Finally, I warmly acknowledge the help given by my wife, Elizabeth, who has provided continuous encouragement during the five years of preparation of this text, and has commented with care and attention on the whole text.

Science and the Bible
Evidence-Based Christian Belief

CHAPTER I

Evidence

TYPES OF EVIDENCE

E VIDENCE is that which is ground for belief. That which is evident can be seen, or is clear to the mind, or is obvious. Probably the most common idea of evidence is in a case at law, and is the basis for a judgment of innocence, guilt, or not proven. A judge or jury is called upon to decide the nature of an act and its cause, and often to decide the intent of the accused. It may not be the sort of evidence that forms the basis for a religious belief, nor are religious beliefs determined by the equivalent of a judge or jury.

The bases for religious belief relate to an inquiring person, seeking answers to questions such as "Who or what made me?" and "For what purpose?" The evidence considered will start from personal experience, deeply influenced by religious beliefs of family and friends. The evidence of the Bible often takes on a central role and its accounts of historical and other events become important features. The main difference from contemporary evidence is the inability to cross-question the sources. This is also the case in considering evidence of other historical events, with documents from a variety of dates and in different languages. Commentaries on the Bible, and discussions of beliefs, will also provide bases for Christian belief.

An important distinction needs to be recognized between oral testimony given by a particular person, together with documents written by individuals or groups of people, and technologically discovered scientific evidence. The experience that lies behind scientific evidence is nearly always available to all suitably qualified people. It too is communicated by oral testimony and documents but appeal can be made by the interested person to the phenomena originally observed. There are, however, some unique or very rare events in nature.

Questions about the universe and its formation are part of the search for religious beliefs, and are increasingly being answered by scientific studies. The nature of a Creator God is clearly revealed, in part, by studies of his Creation. In the last six hundred years tremendous discoveries about the nature of the solar system, the basic laws of physics, the evolution of the physical universe, and the evolution of human beings have been made.

Evidence in science relates mostly to observations and experiments that can be repeated anywhere, at any time, but these usually require considerable expertise and sometimes require expensive equipment. Apparatus is designed to extend the powers of direct human observation. Optical microscopes are well-known instruments, but nowadays for some research it is necessary to supplement them with electron microscopes that are able to show individual molecules. Optical telescopes are supplemented by radio-telescopes, with large arrays of aerials for the highest resolution of stellar objects at extreme distances. Microphones for hearing, chemical apparatus for smell and taste, and pressure-sensitive devices for touch also extend the powers of observation of our five senses. An important characteristic of much modern equipment is the automatic recording of the evidence, relatively free from immediate human interpretation, but requiring subsequent careful evaluation.

One aspect of scientific observations that needs to be brought out into the open is the possibility of being mistaken in what is thought to have been seen or heard. This is such a common experience that, once it is identified as something to be aware of, there is usually little difficulty in devising means to avoid or minimize its dangers, at least in serious science. If you know what you are looking for you are more likely to find it, and if you see something that appears to be "new" it needs further study before it is accepted as important or rejected as spurious.

At a deeper level of physics research, there are particles such as neutrinos that are exceptionally difficult to detect and identify; they can travel from pole to pole of the earth 100,000 million times with only a 50 percent chance of hitting something. The entities known as quarks cannot be observed one by one, but only when bound together in twos or threes. At this point some people ask, "Are such particles real?" This is a particularly relevant question when the particles are hypothetical, some of which are referred to as "virtual" particles, which are vital for the success of new theories. Some critics, both within and outside science, sometimes make much of this and similar questions, which invites the other question, "What is reality?" but I shall not consider such matters in this book.

In a court of law, evidence is submitted by witnesses under oath, who are then open to cross-examination by opposing lawyers. This can be a very demanding experience. By means of penetrating questions, implied distrust, and suggestions of reasonable but untrue alternatives, the task of a jury to determine the "facts" of the case can be made either easier or more difficult, and either way the verdict can be false. Hearsay evidence, statements made out of court by someone not present to testify under oath, is generally excluded in Anglo-American cases, although there are exceptions. One reason for this exclusion is the lack of opportunity to cross-examine the absent person. There are clearly differences between this legal approach to reliable evidence and attempts to establish the reliability of the sort of evidence usually encountered in studies of historical events, and in the reported events and sayings of the Bible and other sacred texts.

Oral evidence usually involves individual experiences of that person and, in contradistinction to scientific evidence, no other person can expect or claim to have the same identical experience. It may be very similar, and be expressed in similar words, but this achieves little of the universality and repeatability of experiences in science. Again, documents available as evidence have been written by one or more individuals and have been influenced by the writer's interpretations, and his or her need to select words to convey that evidence, quite apart from errors in transcription. Ancient documents, such as those used to attempt to establish an agreed text for the books of the New Testament, are often available in several versions with alternative readings, and with omitted or added verses. The evaluation of such evidence is a significant part of biblical scholarship.

In the act of reading documents, in order to establish what the reader considers to be reliable evidence, another layer of individual interpretation enters, in some cases including the difficulties of translations. A great deal of collaborative research may be necessary to reach conclusions that are received and believed by a majority, if indeed such a majority is achievable. This is perhaps nowhere more obvious than in the approach to the Bible and other hallowed writings that are held to be of great importance. The Muslim belief in the need to study Arabic in order to read an agreed text of the Qur'an is easy to appreciate.

The statement "that which is evident can be seen or is clear to the mind" illustrates the need to distinguish between literal and metaphorical interpretations. "Seen" literally means "observed by the eye" but it is also used in relation to the appreciation both of immediate evidence, from whatever source, and conclusions drawn from that evidence, seeing with the mind or the heart. This is a guide and a warning in the evaluation of all sorts of evidence. The use of words that can be taken literally, ambiguously, or metaphorically is common in both theological and scientific statements and can lead to serious disagreements. Evaluation of the meaning of such statements is part of the demanding work of theologians, and spills over into the experience of believers in general. A sensitive appreciation of the richness of metaphor can resolve many of the problems associated with key Christian beliefs.

Scientific documents containing theoretical data and developments have the advantage of including much mathematical material that is almost entirely unambiguous, and most of it is readily understandable by qualified people in all languages. Even so, there remain individual interpretations. Experts do of course sometimes disagree, and further research is needed.

ABSENCE OF EVIDENCE IS NOT EVIDENCE OF ABSENCE

In many situations it is desirable to have more evidence to assist our judgments and consequent decisions. This is particularly so in cases at law where the required decision is "Guilty" or "Not guilty." The use-fulness of an alternative result, "Not proven," as in Scottish law, is then obvious. Sometimes provisional decisions need to be revised when extra evidence, supportive or conflicting, is presented. For those pre-viously declared "Not guilty" it is only recently that this has been con-sidered desirable and legal, although, in the United Kingdom, the Court of Appeal has always been used when circumstances change.

Although it could be said that insufficiency of evidence is endemic in science, it has less serious consequences. Final decisions do not fea-ture in science in the way that they do in cases at law. Scientists are for-ever seeking new evidence, whether to falsify an earlier conclusion or to reinforce earlier observations by repetition or by providing greater accuracy.

Many instances occur in the Bible where we wish there were further evidence. We select one from the Old Testament and one from the New. The clearest example is provided by archaeological studies in Egypt and Palestine relating to David and Solomon. Only in Israel are there references to the name David in archaeological material, and the interpretations of both of the only two items found have been chal-lenged. One, discovered in 1993 at Tel Dan, appears to read "king of Israel" and "king of the house of David," possibly dating from one hun-dred years after the time of David. Another inscription is provided by the famous Moabite stone, in the Louvre, with a cast in the British Museum. It was erected by the Moabite king Mesha about 840 B.C.E. (before the Common Era), and was discovered in 1868, but not authoritatively translated until 1994. This stone was broken into over fifty pieces by Bedouin who distrusted negotiators offering to buy it. Some thirty-eight pieces were subsequently tracked down and a tat-tered paper "squeeze" or "cast," made before the stone was broken, assisted the reassembly and translation. The phrase "house of David" is achieved by inserting the initial "D" of David in a damaged word but there has been disagreement among the archaeologists and Hebrew scholars. The Moabite stone is important as the earliest evidence of the worship of Yahweh. It also provides confirmation of some of the details of historical events in 2 Kings 3:1–7.

The name Solomon has not yet been discovered outside the Bible, in spite of his international claims to fame. His building of the Temple in Jerusalem, (1 Kings 6–7, 2 Chronicles 3–4), an archaeological site that cannot at present be investigated further, and his marriage to a pharaoh's daughter (of unknown name) are absent from the archaeological evidence. There are many contemporary written records from neighboring countries, but not a single reference to the name Solomon.

In both instances the answer may well be that the two kings were known in archaeological records under different names. We note that the name given to Solomon by the Lord through the prophet Nathan was Jedidiah = "Beloved of the Lord" (2 Sam. 12:25). This is known to be a title or royal coronation name, Daduya. The name for David in the el-Amarna tablets, dated 1020–1000 B.C.E., is Tadua, which is the Hurrian (northern Mesopotamian) title or royal/coronation name given to Elhanan (= David) when he became king in 1011 B.C.E. Later it was Hebraized as Dadua and became the biblical David. It is, of course, possible for new archaeological studies to uncover both well-known names Solomon and David.

Some of the stories about David have found convincing archaeological evidence for their trustworthiness but without the actual name David. Excavations in the 1950s led to the discovery of the pool of Gibeon, in unlikely terrain, the place where David conferred with Abner (2 Sam. 2:13), before defeating him in battle. The pool is remarkable—a stone water-shaft cut into bedrock, twelve meters diameter, eleven meters deep. Nearby jar handles, fifty-six of them, were found with the name "Vineyard of Gibeon," dated to about four hundred years after David.

The capture of Jerusalem by David (2 Sam. 5:6–8) in 1005 B.C.E. was via a water-shaft. In 1876 a tunnel was discovered which agreed with the biblical descriptions. In 1961 it was shown to have led inside the city from outside the city walls. Unfortunately, not a single sherd of pottery from the time of David has been discovered near the shaft. There is a gap from the Canaanites in the eighteenth century B.C.E. to Israelites in the eighth century B.C.E. Very few eleventh-century potsherds occur elsewhere.

It has been suggested that the Old Testament history has been exaggerated, or in places invented, to bolster national claims or establish an historical basis for the Jewish religion. It can but be repeated, time and again, "Absence of evidence is not evidence of absence."

Our New Testament example of lack of sufficient evidence concerns the Massacre of the Innocents by Herod, and the flight into Egypt. The murder of the innocents who were less than two years old in and around Bethlehem (Matt. 2:16) seems most improbable as it is not mentioned in other histories, including that of Josephus, who was well aware of Herod's cruelty. The flight into Egypt then comes into question being linked to a theological need, "This was to fulfill what had been spoken by the Lord through the prophet, 'Out of Egypt have I called my son'" (Matt. 2:15 and Hosea 11:1), but again there is no supporting evidence.

FACTS

On many occasions reference will be made to the evidence of science or the accepted evidence of science. There will be numerous well-known examples, such as "the earth is spherical and not flat" and "the earth goes round the sun." I shall use the evidence of science with particular reference to what is accepted by the large majority of scientists, often referred to as "scientific facts." It is worth dwelling for a while on this widespread acceptance of most of what is discovered by science, for it is remarkable that the evidence of science is accepted by nearly all people of every race, religion, political persuasion, language, and whatever kind of distinction one might be led to name. There is no other human activity that leads to such universal agreement.

Some critics of science say you cannot rely on the observations and theories of scientists because they are forever making new observations and theories that contradict or augment the earlier ones. Another word ought perhaps to be added to evidence of science, not just accepted but presently accepted evidence of science. This highlights the danger of believing that presently accepted evidence from science has some absolute and everlasting identity and value. Scientists certainly do not claim such value for their evidence. On the other hand, there are many scientific "facts" that are most unlikely to be changed. The law of gravity propounded by Isaac Newton has never been disproved in innumerable carefully measured events that are commonly encountered, but it is now known that Einstein's theory of relativity is more precise in certain circumstances such as those involving exceptionally high velocities or energies.

The relevance of this becomes clear when we consider what we are going to do with such evidence, especially in relation to beliefs, and to Christian belief in particular. There is nothing to be ashamed of in admitting that science progresses, nor should it inhibit the use of the accepted evidence of science in pursuing our beliefs. Any judge, human or divine, would expect us to use the best evidence available, and to be prepared to reassess our deductions, including our Christian beliefs, in the light of improved evidence. Again, if scientists indicate that their evidence is so unconfirmed that it is unwise to use it to form the basis for our Christian beliefs, then we have a duty to be extra careful in our use of that evidence.

There is a very real sense in which it can be said that science does not prove anything, although it does provide relevant evidence. Repeated observations in a variety of situations that always lead to the same result certainly increase confidence but they do not prove it to be correct in all circumstances. One single new observation, perhaps in slightly different circumstances, can disprove the generally accepted result. This is reflected in the common belief that a proper scientific theory must always be able to be disproved on the basis of its empirical predictions. This disproof can be achieved by new conflicting observations or by mathematical or logical reasoning.

Some scientific results are liable to be dismissed with the comment, "Of course that is only theoretical!" The word "only" suggests that it is a purely theoretical conjecture, but that is very rarely the case. Analyses of relevant observations sometimes lead to theoretical arguments for the existence of, for example, a new kind of nuclear particle. In many important cases these theoretical proposals have led to the particle's discovery in carefully designed experiments. One present-day example is the Higgs particle, which is suggested as the explanation for the masses of particles and has not yet been definitively observed. It is misleading to use the term "theoretical" as if it is less important than direct evidence. Theories that have been exhaustively tested by both experiment and mathematical reasoning, and found to be of value, and especially those that have no competing alternative theories, are surely of great significance. Indeed it is the success of these well-established theories that lends conviction to the use of this theoretical evidence in the shaping of our beliefs.

At this point it is worth recognizing that although scientists have belief in their established theories, they do not cease to try to design experiments to test or disprove some of those theories, knowing that they might have good cause to revise their scientific beliefs in the light of new evidence.

TRUTH

Notice that I have not yet used the word "truth." Ill-considered use of this word leads to many unnecessary arguments. As a first step in the introduction of truth I would plead for the use of at least one adjective, such as scientific truth, or historical truth, or religious truth, or truth decided by a jury. And the same would be to our benefit if corresponding adjectives were also used in relation to evidence—scientific, historical, religious, or legal evidence. I have already indicated that it is clear that present scientific truth is likely to be modified as science gathers more evidence. The same is true of most other kinds of truth, excepting perhaps those claimed to be "absolute" truths that many people find so difficult to accept and to understand when they are given as part of descriptions of religious truth. There is never enough evidence to be totally confident in declaring a truth as "absolute." Such beliefs spring from special study, which is unlikely to be generally available to, or appreciated by, most people. That is not to deny that many people believe in what they would describe as absolute truths without being clear as to the evidence for those absolute beliefs. The question then is "What would they accept as sufficient evidence to cause them to change their beliefs?"

Mathematical truth is sometimes considered to be "absolute," "necessary," or "infallible," but care needs to be exercised in the analysis of the meaning of such claims. We say 2 + 3 equals 5 and believe it to be absolutely true, and in a sense it is "analytically true," but only because that is what we mean by 5. The concepts 2, 3, and 5 are made up of units considered to be equal in every way, although no examples of such units are to be found in our world of experience. The theorem of Pythagoras, with the square on the hypotenuse of a right-angled triangle being equal to the sum of the squares on the other two sides, depends on the assumption that the triangle is on a "flat" surface. It is therefore true, but a special case, and does not apply to spherical geometry with a triangle on the surface of a sphere, or to other "non-Euclidean" geometries. The use of "infinities" of one kind or another, including the "infinitesimals" of differential and integral calculus, leads to deeply fascinating philosophical problems. Such usage has been important in the development of scientific theories that appear to interpret many scientific observations. There seems to be an intriguing connection between the abstract ideas of mathematics and the observed patterns of the physical sciences.

One other use of the word "truth" is of interest—in the phrase "self-evident truth." The best-known example of this is in the American Declaration of Independence, July 4, 1776:

> We hold these truths to be self-evident, that all men are created equal, that they are endowed by their Creator with certain unalienable Rights, that among these are Life, Liberty and the pursuit of Happiness.

The original draft by Thomas Jefferson read,

> We hold these truths to be sacred and undeniable; that all men are created equal and independent, that from that equal creation they derive rights inherent and inalienable, among which are the preservation of life, and liberty, and the pursuit of happiness.

The wordings suggest strongly that these truths are based on religious beliefs. For Cardinal Newman, in his *History of My Religious Opinions to the Year 1833*, there were "two and two only supreme and luminously self-evident beings, myself and my Creator." These usages come close to Plato's belief that all our "ideas" are innate including necessary truths. Descartes considered the idea of God to be innate. Others denied the existence of innate ideas.

CHAPTER 2

Belief

TYPES OF BELIEF

HUMAN BELIEFS over the ages have developed from folk beliefs to the wide variety of philosophical, religious and scientific beliefs of today. Folk beliefs included superstitions, witchcraft, ghosts and mythological creatures, divination, omens, magic, and second sight. They have been studied since the middle of the seventeenth century and, although many are discredited, a few people still find them convincing. Some beliefs based on philosophical analyses of traditional ideas of the nature of the universe and the nature of humans are documented from over four thousand years ago.

The beliefs of humans in all areas of their experience, such as art, music, science, and, in particular, religion, need to be considered. It is not always appreciated that science is based on three beliefs that are also held by religious people. The first is that the universe is sufficiently ordered and stable to make science possible. The second is that people are able, with care, to make reliable observations. The third is that people with sufficient training are able to understand, and hence to propose, theories that allow assessment of the interrelation and significance of such scientific observations.

People who have religious beliefs would probably express these three basic human beliefs somewhat differently. First, the universe is created by a God characterized by Order. Second, God invites us to study his universe, including what it is to be human, with a sense of right and wrong, and he both inspires scientists in their work and reveals religious truths to those who seek. The third belief is closely common to the two fields and emphasizes that all religious beliefs involve understanding and require ideally a sufficient level of education and training to allow the appreciation of the reasons that led to existing doctrines, the formulation of new or revised doctrines, and the recognition of the significance of any proposed revisions.

A prime question is "Should we be prepared to revise our beliefs in all areas of our experience in the light of new knowledge and understanding?" My answer is a resounding "Yes!" Thereby science, the arts and religion are each part of human development, of which there is incontrovertible evidence in history. This includes the evidence of the Old Testament for the shaping of the idea of God by the Jews, and the evidence of the New Testament in the shaping of the Early Church. Even in science the recognition of a significantly new truth usually takes some time to become widely accepted. Einstein developed his theory of special relativity in 1905, the same year in which he explained the photoelectric effect, the emission of electrons from metals by light of a suitable wavelength or color. His powerful theory of general relativity came ten years later. He was awarded the Nobel Prize in Physics in 1921 "for services to the theory of physics, and especially for his discovery of the laws of the photoelectric effect," "independently of such value as may be ultimately attached to his theories of relativity and gravity, if these are confirmed." The first generally accepted confirmation of the general theory was made in 1919, and the observation was repeated in 1922, by measuring, during an eclipse of the sun, the bending of a beam of light from a star by a massive object, the sun.

The efforts of those inclined to disagree with newly or long-accepted theories are of real value, for people are driven to suggest yet more observations or experiments to test the new ideas, and people on both sides of the argument are encouraged to attempt to express their beliefs in the controversial theories in a manner that is persuasive for those who can enter into a reasoned preference. There is no "authoritative body" in science that claims to be able to decide whether or not a theory is "correct." With respect to doctrines in religion it is not uncommon to find claims that a particular doctrine is "correct," or orthodox, with implicit or explicit denial of the value of other doctrines.

REASON

The understanding of theories and doctrines, and the assessment of their significance, involve reasoning. It is in the field of reason that most disagreement arises. At one extreme are those religious believers who would dispense with observation, and deny the value of reason, and would claim that their beliefs were received and recorded in the Bible as direct revelations from God, even including the actual words needed to communicate these revelations to other people. At the other extreme are those who believe that reasoning is all important, and they would not recognize significant personal religious experience, or even some scientific results. Between these two extremes are those, by far the large majority, who respect observations, whether common to other observers or claimed as purely personal, and they exercise reason and inference in the formulation of theories or doctrines that they share with others.

Perhaps the most basic of religious beliefs is that the universe must have been created, and God is the creator. This is unlikely to have been a primeval belief. Natural events were first believed to be influenced by "spirits," and it was some time before multiple gods were succeeded by a single God. There are, however, people with the same scientific and other evidence who are prepared to believe that creation is purely a matter of chance and needs no creator. No amount of pure reason can be confidently expected to change one belief into the other, or the other into the one, positive to negative or negative to positive.

The existence of God cannot be proved, and "absolute" scientific truth cannot be proved. But there is a difference: progress in science is generally believed to be an approach toward "absolute" scientific truth, but progress in Christian belief has to start from a belief in the existence of God, and the progress is in knowledge and understanding based on "theories" of what God is like, what humans are like, and the relationship that occurs.

FAITH

Most Christians will talk about their faith, and some would equate this with their beliefs. But beliefs are not the whole of faith, and need to be related to other aspects of faith, in particular trust and hope, and their outcome in love for God and love of neighbor. It helps some people to think of belief as associated with the mind, trust with the heart, in the nonphysical sense of that word, and hope with the soul, which is most simply thought of as that which survives physical death and for many people has some difficult-to-define association with the present life. (See chapter 12, "Person-Material, Mental, Spiritual.") Beliefs can be based on evidence but may also be based on an accepted authority, or claim to be directly revealed. Trust, which is inseparable from love and linked to providence, implies that God can influence people or events, with or without contradiction of the order in the universe found by scientists. Hope implies not only belief in a temporal future but also the belief that there is some kind of life after death. Trust and hope, in terms of life after death, are not like scientific beliefs, but relate to individuals, usually in the context of community, and their experience of a relationship with their God.

It is fascinating and challenging to consider how new theories, and also new religious doctrines, are formulated. Small changes from existing theories or doctrines cause less surprise than those large shifts in concepts or relationships so familiar in science, and in the history of religion. The role of analogy finds a place here. If waves can act like particles, as found for light, ought not particles to act like waves? This was found to be the case for electrons, first thought of as particles but then found to have wave-like properties. In the development of religious beliefs Christians find the sacrificial killing of a lamb, believed to lead to forgiveness of sins, to have its divine analogy in the understanding that the killing of Jesus, "the Lamb of God" (John 1:29, Rev. 5:6 *et passim*), led to deliverance for those who believe.

The willingness of scientists to change their theories in the face of new evidence or new reasoning contrasts with the practice of most theologians, at least in years gone by, to cling to existing beliefs. It is not easy for new experiences, or a new way of looking at well-known experiences, to give rise to readily acceptable new religious doctrines. The testing of new doctrines, by living through relevant experiences, is rarely part of the recommended activity of believers. Bold are those who are prepared to try, knowing that more than one generation of thought is likely to be required.

A common but not universal test of religious orthodoxy is to see how a belief relates to the earliest known beliefs of the Church, and more particularly to texts and traditions in the Bible. Agreement is rarely widespread in searching for the earliest beliefs, and corresponding texts in the Bible, but the criteria are very influential. There is no such parallel in science, in fact quite the opposite. The latest set of accepted observations and correlating and explaining theories are the contemporary criteria.

CHRISTIAN BELIEF

The "Christian Belief" in our title invites an explanation of what it includes. The phrase "Christian belief" covers three meanings: first, the beliefs that Christians are expected to believe, a filling out of the creeds with related material, and second, beliefs claimed by individual Christians to be directly revealed to them by God. The third meaning of beliefs includes those that some Christians hold that are not a recognizable part of specifically Christian beliefs, but stem from evidence that may have religious implications. An example is the belief that the earth is only six thousand years old, as deduced from the ages of people given in Genesis.

Present-day "churches" and denominations would agree on a large majority of elements of belief and these are fairly easy to discern. All would put some emphasis on the Bible as the basis for Christian belief. Some would accept that knowledge of Creation leads to beliefs about the Creator and the nature of human beings, and such knowledge is mostly derived from science. Many churches have identified creeds that are held to be applicable to the whole Church. There are also statements of belief that relate to individual denominations, sometimes referred to as "Confessions," for example the Lutheran Augsburg Confession (1530) and the Westminster Confession (1646) used by Presbyterians. All start from a belief in a Creator God, and they are convinced of the role of Jesus, the Christ and Messiah who is central to their Christian belief. That Christ is the incarnate Son of God, that he was crucified, and that he rose from the dead is common ground for which the evidence may be examined with confidence. Belief in the Holy Spirit completes the Trinity of Father, Son, and Holy Spirit, as emphasized in baptism.

The Apostles' Creed begins "I believe in God." In Latin this is "*Credo in Deum,*" and the use of the accusative case rather than the dative makes it mean "believing in" or "trusting" as distinct from "believing that." Many today feel it is preferable to use a form found in recent baptismal statements, "I believe and trust in Him." The original so-called Nicene Creed, which is in Greek, opens with "*pisteuomen eis ena Theon,*" "We believe in One God," again using the accusative. In both creeds there is, of course, the belief implicit that there is a God, and in the Nicene Creed it is more explicit, namely that there is (only) one God. But the emphasis is on trusting, not just "believing that . . ." The singular "I" relates to the baptism candidate. The plural "We" is more appropriate for congregational worship.

The Apostles' Creed, first so-named at the synod of Milan in 390 C.E., was accepted at the Council of Nicea (325 C.E.). It was developed from the Baptismal Creed of the Roman Church in the first half of the second century, using earlier material. It was generally recognized at the Reformation, and as given in the *Catechism of The Book of Common Prayer* (final version 1662) declares;

> I believe in God the Father Almighty, Maker of heaven and earth:
>
> And in Jesus Christ, His only Son, our Lord, Who was conceived by the Holy Ghost, Born of the Virgin Mary, Suffered under Pontius Pilate, Was crucified, dead and buried: He descended into hell; The third day he rose again from the dead; He ascended to heaven, And sitteth at the right hand

of God the Father Almighty; From thence he shall come to judge the quick and the dead;

I believe in the Holy Ghost; the holy Catholick Church; The Communion of Saints; The Forgiveness of sins; The Resurrection of the body, And the life everlasting.

The Apostles' Creed in the recent Anglican *Book of Common Worship* (2000) is closely similar, with "creator" for "Maker," "Holy Spirit" for "Holy Ghost," "descended to the dead" for "descended into hell," and "living" for "quick."

The Nicene Creed was the first creed to be published by an Ecumenical Council (Nicea, 325 C.E.). The Council was convened by Constantine, the first Christian emperor, in order to sort out the christological disagreements that were disturbing the empire. It is a carefully revised version of the Creed of Caesarea, presented by Eusebius. After a lively debate, much influenced by Greek theological terminology (see p. 25), it was agreed that Jesus was "of the same substance" (*homoousios*) with God, or "one in being," rather than "of like substance" (*homoiousios*). The school of Alexandria tended to emphasize the divinity of Christ, considered to be of central importance for an understanding of salvation, and the school of Antioch gave emphasis to the humanity of Christ and his moral example. Arian beliefs, such as "There was a time when the Son was not," were carefully repudiated.

The second Ecumenical (or General) Council was held at Constantinople in 381, and its creed, known as the Niceno-Constantinopolitan Creed, has been accepted as authoritative in East and West alike, and is so even today. This creed, with the misnomer "Nicene," is given in the Holy Communion service of the *Book of Common Prayer*:

I believe in one God the Father Almighty, Maker of heaven and earth, And of all things visible and invisible:

And in one Lord Jesus Christ, the only-begotten Son of God, Begotten of his Father before all worlds, God of God, Light of Light, Very God of very God, Begotten, not made, Being of one substance with the Father, By whom all things were made: Who for us men and for our salvation came down from heaven, And was incarnate by the Holy Ghost of the Virgin Mary, And was made man, And was crucified also for us under Pontius Pilate. He suffered and was buried, And the third day he rose again according to the Scriptures, And ascended into heaven, and Sitteth on the right hand of the Father. And he shall come again with glory to judge both the quick and the dead: Whose kingdom shall have no end.

And I believe in the Holy Ghost, the Lord and giver of life, Who proceedeth from the Father and the Son, Who with the Father and the Son together is worshipped and glorified, Who spake by the Prophets. And I believe one Catholick and Apostolick Church. I acknowledge one Baptism for the remission of sins. And I look for the Resurrection of the dead, And the life of the world to come.

The Nicene Creed in the recent Anglican *Book of Common Worship* (2000) has "We" instead of "I," following the authentic Greek text. It also has a number of changes from the wording in the Book of Common Prayer, "of all that is seen and unseen," the "only Son of God, eternally begotten of the Father," "God from God," "true God from true God" "of one being with the Father," "incarnate from the Holy Spirit and the Virgin Mary," and "is seated at the right hand of the Father," "living" for "quick," "Holy Spirit" for "Holy Ghost," "one holy catholic and apostolic Church," and "forgiveness" for "remission." These changes appear small, but some of them have specific doctrinal significance.

Continuing debate about some of the implications of the wording of creeds led to the fourth Ecumenical Council, the Council of Chalcedon (451 C.E.), with 630 bishops. The decisions of Nicea and Constantinople referring to the creed were confirmed. Since Chalcedon, the only significant change has been the insertion in the Western Church of the phrase "and the Son" (*filioque*) after "I believe in the Holy Ghost, the Lord and giver of life, Who proceedeth from the Father." The main "proof text" is John 20:22, "he [i.e. the Son, Jesus] breathed on them and said to them, 'Receive the Holy Spirit.'" The word *filioque* was added by the Council of Toledo in 589 C.E., was slowly adopted, never ratified by a general council, and has been repudiated to this day by the Eastern Church mainly because it appears to compromise the Eastern belief in the primacy of the Father as the source of deity. (See p. 26.)

The phrase was agreed, in principle, not to be essential by the Anglican Lambeth Conference of 1978, and in the recent Anglican *Book of Common Worship* (2000, p. 140) an alternative text of the Nicene Creed is given with the omission of "and the Son." It has been dropped from the revised Eucharist creed in the Canadian Alternative Services (1985, p. 189), but remains in the 1662 version in the same volume (p. 234). The Methodist Conference in 1990 "expressed its willingness to restore the Nicene Creed to the form agreed by East and West in 381 C.E., if and when, in the judgment of the Conference, there is sufficient ecumenical agreement to such a policy in the Western Church."

THE HOLY SPIRIT

There is an essential place in the early Christian preaching for the Spirit of God, also called the Holy Ghost, or the Holy Spirit. Jesus was "anointed" by the Spirit, the disciples at Pentecost received the Holy Spirit, and for the first time Gentiles were seen to receive the same Spirit. This was not understood as the addition of a separate element to the person, but a fulfilling of the spiritual potential of the recipient. There was also a recognition that the members of the "Church" shared the same Spirit. The evidence for the action of the Spirit is, in one sense, known uniquely by the believer in question, but most Christians would claim that they are aware of the action of the Spirit in others, as well as in themselves. Paul's account in 1 Corinthians 12 is used frequently for the encouragement of a variety of "spiritual gifts." Arguments against belief in the activities of the Holy Spirit are generally ineffective, and they founder on such analogies as the claim that the critics are blind, whereas the believers have sight.

The phenomenon of speaking in tongues, frequent in the early Church, and having a modified revival in the late twentieth century, is very much part of group activity. Speaking in tongues, or *glossolalia*, is reported, with two meanings: "All of them were filled with the Holy Spirit and began to speak in other languages, as the Spirit gave them ability" (Acts 2:4), and "we hear, each of us, in our own native language" (Acts 2:8), as if one speaker was understood by people of a variety of languages. This latter meaning seems to lie behind Paul's mention of one of the many gifts of the Spirit in 1 Cor. 12:4–11, including "various kinds of tongues, to another the interpretation of tongues" (v. 10). In 1 Cor. 14:2–19 Paul expands on this topic with a critical emphasis, "for those who speak with a tongue do not speak to other people but to God, for nobody understands them" (v. 2), and finishes with a flourish (vv. 18, 19): "I thank God that I speak in tongues more than all of you; nevertheless, in church I would rather speak five words with my mind, in order to instruct others also, than ten thousand words in a tongue." Interpreters are essential (vv. 20–33).

THE TRINITY

This characteristic belief of Christians finds a clear expression in the Apostles' Creed, "I believe in God the Father . . . in Jesus Christ, His only Son, . . . and in the Holy Ghost," and similarly in the Nicene Creed, "I believe in one God the Father . . . in one Lord Jesus Christ, the only-begotten Son of God, . . . and in the Holy Ghost." The threeness of divinity is found in a number of places in the New Testament, and the words that are found to be helpful in describing each of the three evolved over the first five centuries and became embedded in attempts to describe the relationships between the members of the Trinity. This is most evident in the Nicene Creed in such phrases as "(Jesus Christ) begotten of his Father before all worlds, God of God, Light of Light, Very God of very God, Begotten not made, Being of one substance with the Father, By whom all things were made," and "(the Holy Ghost) the Lord and giver of life, Who proceedeth from the Father and the Son, Who together with the Father and the Son is worshiped and glorified."

It is not possible in the context of this book to provide the wealth of evidence, based on speculation, revelation, and subsequent reasoning, for those creedal beliefs. I shall list some of the New Testament passages that give evidence of the Trinitarian beliefs of the writers of the epistles. There is also the very explicit penultimate verse of Matthew (28:19), "Go therefore and make disciples of all nations, baptizing them in the name of the Father and of the Son and of the Holy Spirit." Many scholars question the authenticity of this verse, but it does link back to Matthew 3 where the Son is baptized (v. 16), the Father speaks (a voice from heaven, 3:17), and the Spirit of God descends (3:16).

The grace in the closing verse of 2 Corinthians (13:13) is used even today, "The grace of the Lord Jesus Christ, the love of God, and the communion [or fellowship] of the Holy Spirit be with all of you." This is one of the earliest epistles, perhaps thirty years after the crucifixion, and has a supporting passage in 1:21–22, "It is God who establishes us with you in Christ and has anointed us, by putting his seal on us and giving us his Holy Spirit in our hearts, as a first installment." Paul's earlier letter to the Corinthians (12:4–6) reads, "Now there are varieties of gifts, but the same Spirit, and there are varieties of services, but the same Lord; and there are varieties of activities, but it is the same God who activates all of them in everyone." A similar trinity of divine beings (or "persons") is recognized in Gal. 4:6, "God has sent the Spirit of his Son into our hearts."

These passages all refer to the times after the Incarnation, but it is possible to identify three "personifications" of God in the Old Testament, namely Wisdom, the Word of God, and the Spirit of God. Wisdom is always female, pre-existent, as in Sir. (Ecclesiasticus) 24:9, "Before the ages, in the beginning, he created me, and for all the ages I shall not cease to be." The Word of God is found in Ps. 119:89, "The Lord exists for ever, your word is firmly fixed in heaven," and in Isa. 55:11, "my word shall accomplish that which I purpose." The Spirit of God is promised to Israel on their return from exile, Ezek. 37:14, "I will put my spirit within you, and you shall live." However, these three personifications do not correlate closely with the Trinity of the New Testament.

Tertullian (160–220), described as "the creator of ecclesiastical

Latinity," introduced many hundreds of new Latin words to assist his thinking. He coined the word *Trínitas* (= Trinity), and used *Substantia* (= substance) to indicate the common unity among the members of the Trinity. Perhaps overconfidently, he used *Persona* (= Person) to translate the Greek word *hypostasis*. Literally *persona* means a "mask," as used to be worn to show the role an actor is playing. Literally *hypostasis* means "substance." The potential confusion caused by the apparent equation of person and substance was suffered by both the Greeks and the Romans. In 362, at the Council of Alexandria, under the influence of Athanasius, agreement was reached between West and East. The Greek *hypostasis* was equated with *persona,* and the Latin *substantia* was equated with the Greek *ousía.* The outcome was the phrase of Tertullian—*una Substantia, tres Personae;* one substance and three persons; one *substantia* or *ousía* and three *hypostases* or *personae.* This is still the accepted way of referring to the Trinity. At the same Council the divinity of the Holy Spirit was identified, a topic that had not been considered at Nicea.

For over one hundred years there were disagreements between Arians of various kinds who followed the belief of Arius (c. 250–336) that Jesus was more than a mere man but less than God. Conflicting quotations from the Bible did not really help; in John 10:30, "The Father and I are one," and John 14:28, "the Father is greater than I." The words of Jesus (John 8:42), "I came from God," were countered by Paul's assertion that all things were "from God" (1 Cor. 8:6, 2 Cor. 5:18). Arius was a popularizer, arguing that the Son was the first of God's creatures. (Col. 1:15, "the firstborn of all creation"). He stirred up the people with slogans such as "Once was when he wasn't," "ἦν ποτε 'ότε ουκ ἦν" (pronounced "een potty hotty ook een").

It is not very difficult to present some of the vocabulary, newly invented or adopted, for discussion of the Trinity. It is, on the other hand, not easy to understand exactly what the words mean. One of the first steps was to come to an agreement that the Father and the Son were "of the same substance" (*homoousios*) and not just "of like substance" (*homoiousios*). Neither of these two Greek words is found in the New Testament. In NRSV the word *ousia* is translated in Luke 15:12–13 as "property" ("substance" in RV) which can be shared and squandered, as by the Prodigal Son.

There remains, even today, a difference between the East and the West in their overall view of relationships in the Trinity. For the West, the Father "begets" the Son, and Father and Son together "breathe" the Holy Spirit. For the East, the Father "begets" the Son, and the Father "breathes" the Holy Spirit. These pictures lie behind the disagreement about the *filioque* (p. 21).

The Athanasian Creed or *Quicunque vult* (Whosoever will be saved . . .) was not referred to at Chalcedon in 451 C.E., although probably extant at that time, being first quoted in 542 C.E. It is a Latin hymn of Western origin and is much concerned to define the belief in the Trinity. It finds a place in the Anglican *Book of Common Prayer,* at Morning Prayer. The Athanasian Creed is one of the seven "Authorized Affirmations of Faith" for use in services of the *Book of Common Worship* (2001, p. 143) of the Anglican Church, and is in the form given in the *Book of Common Prayer.*

The year 362 is significant not only as the date of the Council of Alexandria, with its substantial agreement between East and West, but also as the year in which Julian (the Apostate) became emperor of Rome and declared himself a pagan. He attempted to restore worship to many gods, while declaring universal freedom for toleration of all religions. He even attempted to rebuild the Temple in Jerusalem but flames are said to have burst forth from the foundations and the work was abandoned. In 363 Julian died. His actions showed that beliefs of Christians could not be overcome by providing alternative beliefs, and the dependence of the Christian religion on the State was not essential.

The detailed reasonings leading to beliefs decided in the councils and the Reformation are many and wide-reaching. My emphasis is on evidence of events and personal and collective experiences, and their interpretation. Within the Church there is a wide and rich spectrum of beliefs and a seeker after the truth delivered by Jesus, and by the "Spirit of Truth," needs to decide how far to go in searching. At one extreme are those who, without question, accept the formularies of a given body of believers, and at the other extreme are those who wish to study each and every belief before choosing their own panoply of conviction and comfort. As human beings with free will, and a determination to worship the Lord our God with all our mind, as Jesus commanded (Matt. 22:37), and with all our heart and soul, Christians have a clear duty to respect all honest attempts of seekers, of whatever religion, wherever they are on their pilgrimage.

CHAPTER 3

Evidence in the Bible

THE TEXT OF THE BIBLE

THERE ARE SO MANY translations of the Bible available today, in any one language, that it is not possible to find one version that commands recognition by the majority of readers. The first translation into English was from the Latin, by John Wycliffe in 1382. William Tyndale translated the New Testament from the Greek in 1525. Of English texts available today, the one adhered to most tenaciously by a limited number of people is the Authorized Version of 1611 (AV). It was not until 1880–85 that it was taken as the basis for the Revised Version (RV). Each of these translations used a contemporary assessment of the available Hebrew, Greek, Latin, and other texts, based on the opinions of many respected scholars. These opinions have been augmented and modified by subsequent discoveries and studies, and modern translators exercise considerable freedom in producing new versions, each with their own starting text and implicit or explicit intentions. I shall quote from the New Revised Standard Version (NRSV, 1995), as used for references in the Anglican Common Worship (2001), although "any version of Holy Scripture which is not prohibited by lawful authority may be used" for the readings.

As an example of the variety of English translations encountered, it is instructive to look at the word "saints." I have studied its use in the AV (1611), and then in the same verses in the RV (1880) and eight other versions.[1] It is helpful to consider the Bible in four sections, the Gospels, the rest of the New Testament (NT), the Psalter, and the rest of the Old Testament (OT).

In the Four Gospels there is only one verse with "saints," namely Matt. 27:52, referring to the tombs opening after the death of Jesus when "many bodies of the saints that had fallen asleep were raised." This usage of "saints" is found only in the AV, RV, Revised English Bible (REB), and NRSV, and some question the authenticity of this verse. In the rest of the New Testament there are fifty-six uses of "saints" in AV, fifty-five in the Jerusalem Bible (JB), fifty-four in the RV, fifty-three in the NRSV, and thirty-nine in the New International Version (NIV). In the five other texts there are none. Curiously, the translation of *díkaion*, in Matt. 23:29, normally taken as "righteous," is given as "saints" in the New English Bible (NEB) and the REB, but not in the other versions studied. There may be other examples of the introduction of "saints" in one or more versions by varying the normal translation of words such as *díkaion*.

In the Psalter, only the AV, RV, and NIV use "saints." In the rest of the Old Testament, the uses are twelve in the AV, six in the RV, five in the NIV, and three in the JB (all in Daniel), other versions being zero. Only one individual is explicitly given the title "saint," "Aaron the saint of the Lord" (Ps. 106:16), in the AV and RV, but not in other translations.

Only one Greek word is normally translated as "saint" (*hagios*, plural *hagioi*), from which we get the word *hagiography* for a book of the lives of the saints. As an adjective it is translated "holy" and its primary meaning is "separated or dedicated to God." It has close association with other Greek words that mean "pure" (*hagnos*) and "religious awe" (*hagos*). Two Hebrew words are translated as "saints"—the plurals Qaddish and Hasidim. Both can be translated as "holy," the latter almost exclusively for people, the former more widely for people and objects such as garments and vessels.

The several alternative translations for "saints" include "holy ones," "devout ones," "faithful ones," "loyal servants," "God's people," "those who are devoted to him," and "holy men." The statistics reported here are evidence of the decision in JB and NRSV to restrict the use of the word "saints" to Christians, on every one of over fifty occasions. In verses where the AV uses "saints," the Good News Bible (GNB) and NEB never use "saints" in the whole Bible, and the REB uses it only twice.

The titles of the Gospels in the AV call the authors "St." Most epistles in the AV are by "Paul the Apostle," including Romans and Hebrews, but Paul to Titus, Paul to Philemon, and James, Peter, John, and Jude are names without a title. The final book is headed "The Revelation of St. John the Divine." The RV follows the same pattern but uses "S" instead of "St." Five other versions omit "St." and "S" from the titles of the Gospels.[2] All the versions, except the NIV, assign the usual epistles to Paul, but four versions exclude this assignment to Hebrews.[3] The canonization of saints has been criticized in some branches of the Church and has without doubt influenced translations of the Bible issuing from or directed toward Christians in those traditions.

Thus the starting point in using the Bible, whether in the accepted "original," that is, ancient texts, or in translation, has a degree of uncertainty. This is not meant to undermine the value of the texts. It is a warning against overenthusiastic quotations and arguments, especially when differences of opinion are directly related to differences of text or translation.

Some people place great emphasis on attempts to find the earliest or most reliable text of the Bible, as if that would be the only one truly representative of the divine revelation. A more open approach is to see the variations as evidence of mistaken memory, or miscopying, or of limited attempts to clarify the meaning, or of deliberate changes to match more closely the interpretation favored by the scribe. It would be very surprising to find one single "orthodox" text among groups with such different backgrounds of beliefs and practices. However, some 90 percent of the NT sources agree with each other, and seldom do the differences affect traditional Christian beliefs.

Recent Discoveries
of Ancient Manuscripts

Relatively recent discoveries of ancient manuscripts contribute significantly to attempts to establish early versions of the texts. The *Dead Sea Scrolls* were discovered in caves near Qumran, in Israel, on the northwest corner of the Dead Sea, from 1947 onwards. Nine hundred

Aramaic and Hebrew texts include 225 biblical scrolls, with two almost complete copies of Isaiah, and fragments of every OT book in the familiar sequence, but with the absence of Esther. These scrolls were written between about 200 B.C.E. and the time of their secret deposition in 68 C.E. and are therefore some 1,000 years older than any other known Hebrew texts. There are fragments of forty separate manuscripts of the Psalms, thirty of Deuteronomy, and twenty-one of Isaiah, showing the importance given to these books. The same three books are quoted most frequently in the New Testament. Many variant readings, omissions and additions are found. Various other texts appear to have come from a previously unknown Jewish community, probably related to the Essenes.

Another important find was made at Nag Hammadi in Egypt in 1945, in an earthenware jar. One of fifty-two books, it is known as the *Gospel of Thomas*, dating from the second century C.E. The book is not in the form of the usual scroll but on double-sided parchment sheets. It contains 114 sayings of Jesus in Coptic, probably translated from the Greek, which in turn was a translation of the Aramaic that Jesus spoke. More than half of the sayings have close parallels to those in the Four Gospels, but with significant variations and additions. It is important to see the influence of Greek thought on sections of the Early Church, and these parallel other writings labeled as "Gnostic," but avoid the extreme dualism of some Gnostic traditions. The sayings claim to have "hidden" meanings for those who can understand.

THE "MISSING" BOOK OF JASHAR

There are two references in the Old Testament to the Book of Jashar. In Josh. 10:12–13 it is recorded how Joshua

> said in the sight of Israel, Sun, stand still at Gibeon, and Moon, in the valley of Aijalon. And the sun stood still, and the moon stopped, and the nation took vengeance on their enemies (the Amorites). Is this not written in the Book of Jashar? The sun stopped in mid-heaven, and did not hurry to set for about a whole day.

After the defeat of the Israelites, we read in 2 Sam. 1:17–18 that "David intoned this lamentation over Saul and his son Jonathan. (He ordered that The Song of the Bow be taught to the people of Judah; it is written in the Book of Jashar.)"

The Book of Jashar appeared in a variety of versions in the nineteenth century, and a sixteenth-century English copy was rediscovered in the archives of Rouen Cathedral in 1929 and obtained by the Bibliothèque Nationale in Paris. An American historian, Michael Martin of Philadelphia University, examined it in 1993, researched its history, and published the manuscript of the Book of Jashar in 1995. He concluded that a scroll containing the book was seized by the Babylonian king Nebuchadnezzar when he captured Jerusalem in 597 B.C.E. It was looted by the Persian king Cyrus II when he captured Babylon in 539 B.C.E., and remained in the great library of Gazna in Persia until it was bought by Alcuin, the English abbot of Tours, during a pilgrimage about 800 C.E. It was translated into Latin in the 1140s and copied into English during the sixteenth century and taken to Rouen. Hitherto such claims for authenticity of medieval and recent versions have been rejected, one opinion being that they are an "impudent forgery," and there is a need for this new evidence to be put on a firmer footing.

The book in question has no chapters or verses, as was the custom for the older versions of OT books. It covers the period spent by the Israelites in the wilderness, with comments on earlier events. The book says that Jashar was the successor of Moses and he appointed Joshua as the army field commander. Israel is the name given to Abraham, not to Jacob. The book tells how, when Jacob and his family moved into Egypt, Esau remained in Edom. It is probably in Edom that Moses encountered God and was told to deliver the Israelites from Egypt. One striking feature is that Jashar is described as the high priest of Bethel, where Baal, the storm god, was worshipped, which was regarded as a competitor of the Jerusalem Temple. This, and the discrepancies between Jashar and the accepted versions of events, may explain why the book was omitted from the approved collection of books, probably in the time of Josiah (640–609 B.C.E.).

THE NEW TESTAMENT

In the search for evidence on which to base Christian belief, the New Testament has a unique value. It is a collection of twenty-seven books, namely the Four Gospels, the Acts of the Apostles, twenty-one letters of Paul and others, and Revelation. It is supported by over 5,000 manuscripts, complete, partial or fragmentary, the oldest being a fragment of John's Gospel dated 120–140 C.E. Further support comes from quotations in the writings of early Christians. Before the contents of the New Testament were clearly defined, up to fifty gospels appear to have circulated. The first attempt to define the officially recognized books, known as the "canon," of the New Testament began about 150 C.E. The first use of the technical word "Canon" was by Athanasius in 352 C.E. By the time of the Muratori "Canon" (a fragment discovered by the Italian Muratori in 1740), dated about 200 C.E., twenty books were recognized. The first appearance of the present list of twenty-seven books was given by Athanasius in 367 C.E.

The events in the Gospels, however, are not in a determined and consistent historical sequence, and to see the relation between them it is necessary to set out the first three in parallel columns, with some passages reordered. What then becomes remarkable is the very close agreement in the three texts for many sayings, parables, and events. Closer study suggests strongly that Mark, which is the shortest, is the earliest, and was used by Matthew and Luke. Both Matthew and Luke appear to have access to supplementary material, some of which is common to these two Gospels. This has led to the suggestion that they used a common source, referred to as Q, from the German word *Quelle*, meaning source. The historian and theologian Eusebius of Caesarea (c. 260–340 C.E.) developed an ingenious system to assist the reader, dividing the text into sections relating to parallels in other Gospels, and this was adopted in many manuscripts.

John's Gospel is easily recognized as different in style, thought, and emphasis. It is a coherent drama, with a prologue (chapter 1), two main acts (chapters 2–12, 13–20), and an epilogue (chapter 21). Its main theological themes are expressed metaphorically as "life," "light," and "glory." Jewish and Greek religious ideas are combined in a manner reminiscent of some of the Dead Sea Scrolls and the *Gospel of Thomas*. Although some scholars feel that there are elements of Gnosticism in John's Gospel (see p. 48), Gnostic words such as faith, wisdom, knowledge, nature (*physis*), spiritual, mystery, apocalypse (revelation), and image are absent. It has been suggested that the delay in accepting John's Gospel into the Canon was because of doubts about its orthodoxy, including its possible relation to Gnosticism, and it may even have been edited to remove such words. It has been claimed to be independent of the first three Gospels, but it is easy to believe that at the time when it was written the author was aware of the Gospels of Mark, Matthew and Luke, and yet declined to use them to any great extent.

Having set out the pedigree and some of the characteristics of the New Testament, it is now possible to make tentative comments about the evidence it affords for Christian belief both in its overall emphasis and in relation to individual events and specific doctrines.

The commonly accepted and recommended approach is to start with the text, read it, digest it, and then ask questions. For the nonspecialist, especially one for whom the text is largely unknown, one early question is "What shall I do about apparently contradictory sayings, or incompatible accounts of events?" An encouraging reply would be "Set them on one side for the time being, unless they seem to be central issues." Many of the ethical and moral teachings are usually found to be attractive for both believers and others. Today's inquisitive teenagers and others will ask nagging questions about the miracles, and the divine and human nature of Jesus, and above all about the events and meaning of the crucifixion and resurrection of Jesus. These are at the heart of Christian beliefs. Later chapters will consider most of these points.

THE OLD TESTAMENT

'Testament" is Latin for the Greek *diatheke,* which can mean "will" or "covenant" (Heb. 9:15ff.), a binding relationship between God and humans, or between two groups or individuals. The Old Covenant was based on promises by God and commitments by his chosen people, sealed by various rites. The New Testament shows a new relationship for those committed to Jesus, a covenant seen by Paul as sealed by the death of Jesus, for all humankind.

The Old Testament is a collection of thirty-nine books and constitutes the scriptures of Judaism. Its inclusion in the Bible together with the New Testament indicates and emphasizes the continuity of the history of God's revelation as seen by the Early Church. These scriptures had been translated into Greek at the request of Ptolemy II (285–246 B.C.E.), and became known as the Septuagint, or LXX, a name that indicates the traditional belief that the translation was made by seventy-two (or seventy?) elders, in seventy-two (or seventy?) days. It was regarded as divinely inspired and even claimed as superior to the Hebrew original—almost all NT quotations of the Old Testament are from the Septuagint. The earliest manuscripts are from Qumran and are dated to the second century B.C.E. The Apocrypha, which is not part of the Bible for Jews or for some Protestant Christians, consists of writings found in the Septuagint but not in the traditional Hebrew canon. Seven of the Apocrypha books are included in the Roman Catholic, Greek, and Slavonic Bibles. In the Jerusalem Bible the forty-six books include five Pentateuch, sixteen Historical books, seven Wisdom books, and eighteen Prophets, in a revised order. The Hebrew Bible for Jews, known as the Tanakh, has five books of Moses, six of the Former Prophets, fifteen of the Latter Prophets, and thirteen of the Writings, a total of thirty-nine books.

The prime importance of the Old Testament in relation to Christian belief is its contribution to the understanding of the thoughts and traditions and teaching of Jesus and the Early Church. Jesus and the early Christians were Jews, steeped in the history, rites, practices, and teaching of Judaism, yet showing a marked and explicit degree of independence and even opposition.

The narratives in the Old Testament are stories or histories of the believed actions of God in human events. Most show signs of having been handed down through many generations, together with genealogies, and often indicate the origin of place names and practices. The poetry of the Psalms has a beauty and persuasion typical of Hebrew writing in its most inspired and timeless form. It is composed in praise of God, of his Creation, and of his marvelous works. The Prophets likewise set a pattern that is characteristically individual and rich in forward-looking ideas. Apocalyptic writings (from the Greek *apokalupsis,* for "revealing" or "uncovering") are claimed to be divine disclosures made by angels, dreams, and visions. The clearest example is the Book of Daniel, which is written in two languages, Hebrew and Aramaic, suggesting two authors. It was the last book of the Old Testament to be written and is one of the few OT books that can be dated precisely, between 167 and 163 B.C.E.

Laws and ordinances form a significant part of the Old Testament, and range from the time-honored universal Ten Commandments (Exod. 20:2–17) to the Holiness Code (Leviticus 17–26) for ritual purity and holiness. The laws of Deuteronomy 12 to 26 are presented as if they were spoken by Moses. It is now agreed that they relate to the cultic reforms of King Josiah of Judah (640–609 B.C.E.), particularly in relation to the sacrificial system in the Temple in Jerusalem. The daily life of the Jews, with symbols, requirements. and rules centered on the Temple, with the High Priest entering once a year into the Holy of Holies.

NOTES

1. The New English Bible (NEB, 1961), The Jerusalem Bible (JB, 1966), Holy Bible, The New International Version (NIV, 1973), The Good News Bible (GNB, 1976), The Liturgical Psalter (LP, 1976) as used in the Alternative Service Book (ASB, 1980), The Revised English Bible (REB, 1989), and NRSV (1989, 1995).

2. NEB, NIV, GNB, REB, and NRSV.

3. NEB, GNB, REB, and NRSV.

CHAPTER 4

Interpretation of the Bible

JEWISH INTERPRETATION OF THE
OLD TESTAMENT

THE "SCRIPTURES" referred to by Jesus and the early disciples, and recognized by his hearers, were identical with the Hebrew scriptures of Jewish communities. These were essentially the Old Testament, plus the books now gathered together in the Apocrypha. The Greek translation of the scriptures, the Septuagint, was used by the Diaspora, the Jews scattered over much of the ancient world. The epistles of both James and 1 Peter are specifically addressed to "the twelve tribes of the Dispersion" and "the exiles of the Dispersion." The Septuagint attracted "commentaries" such as those found at Qumran, which explicitly stated "the interpretation of the matter is . . ." and thereby the scriptures were related to the needs of the time. The *midrashim*, expositions and commentaries produced from 70 C.E. onward by rabbinic schools, make clear their reasoning and quote divergent views of various scholars.

It is important to distinguish between *exegesis*, seeking ideas that can be read out of a text, and *eisegesis*, suggesting ideas that can be read into a text. The latter is a central feature of the Jewish tradition, although it is made to look like exegesis, in order to preserve the belief that the canon of scripture is closed, since prophecy was taken to have ceased about the time of the Book of Ezra, between 540 and 440 B.C.E.

A parallel belief that scripture is the word of God exists, with Moses acting simply as a scribe receiving dictation, and "the spirit of prophecy" speaking through the prophets. This led to the treatment of scripture as free from error, with the literal meaning taken as its primary sense. The "literal meaning" used by "literalists" demands extra care when the text is in verse, contains poetic imagery, or uses unfamiliar contemporary ideas. Scripture was also regarded as free from contradictions, and the commentaries tried to prove that apparent contradictions were not real, or that both could be true. The scriptures were considered to be eternally relevant and could never become obsolescent or superseded. Every minute detail could be significant, including the computation of the numerical values of words and phrases and the identification of possible acronyms. Repetitions were studied to discover nuances, and the contexts of verses were carefully assessed. Rabbinic exegesis was used to reinforce the maintenance of long-standing tradition and was aimed at resolving apparent differences in the *halaka* or religious laws.

Philo of Alexandria (15 B.C.E.–50 C.E.), the Jewish scholar influenced by Hellenism, was less committed than the rabbis to the belief that scripture was unalterable, and claimed that his interpretations were divinely inspired. He gave examples of single verses, each of which could have a number of interpretations. Later searches for the meanings and grammar of words, begun in the eighth century, were followed by twelfth-century moves toward allegorical interpretations, in the context of contemporary philosophical points of view, notably by Maimonides (1135–1204), with Aristotelian emphases. His leaning on the "latent" as distinct from the "apparent" sense in scripture bore fruit a century later, when interest developed in esoteric mysticism, Kabbala, which some claimed, following the Gnostics, enabled direct communication with God. The first radical break in Jewish tradition was made by Baruch Spinoza (1632–77), who used a critical, historical approach to the Bible, influenced in part by his scientific achievements, thereby leading to so-called higher criticism. Rabbinic exegesis was continued in the Jewish tradition down to modern times, and Hebrew rabbis and writers were much consulted by Christian scholars. Later Jewish academic scholarship often differed from interpretations favored by Christian contemporaries.

CHRISTIAN INTERPRETATION OF THE BIBLE

Early Christian approaches to interpretation were similar to those of contemporary Jewish scholars. Many features of early Jewish expositions and interpretations of Hebrew scriptures have parallels in Christian interpretations of both Old and New Testaments, especially among literalists and later among fundamentalists. Fundamentalism is a twentieth-century theological movement, largely in North America. Fundamentalists emphasize the "authority" of the Bible, which is believed to be totally free from error, reject modern criticism of the Bible, and stress personal piety and holiness. Claims are made for scripture as a source of doctrinal certainty and of moral absolutes.

Jesus himself emphasized the continuity between the Old and the New Testaments when, after reading Isa. 61:1–2 in the synagogue, he said, "Today this scripture has been fulfilled in your ears" (Luke 4:21). The appeal to prophecy was a major part of the declaration of the new revelation in Jesus, who was seen as a rabbinical teacher. Paul developed the NT practice whereby events in the Old Testament were interpreted as a type or prefiguring of happenings in the Christian church, for example, in 1 Cor. 10:2 "all were baptized into Moses in the cloud and in the sea." OT figures portrayed by the prophets also acted as types or anticipations—the Messianic predictions and the Suffering Servant of Isaiah are claimed to be fulfilled in Jesus.

Allegorical interpretation seeks to reveal underlying meanings present in a text, interpretations of which the author may not have been consciously aware but nevertheless was able to prefigure without seeing how his words might come to be understood by Christians. Thus a narrative can be understood symbolically, with a meaning parallel to but distinct from a literal meaning and brings out a more important implication. It was used by Paul who was "brought up [in Tarsus] at the feet of Gamaliel, educated strictly according to our ancestral law" (Acts 22:3). Thus in Gal. 4:22–26 he refers to the Genesis story of Abraham's sons born to a free woman, Sarah, and a slave woman, Hagar. "Now this is an allegory: these women are two covenants. One woman, in fact, is Hagar, from Mount Sinai, bearing children for slavery…corresponds to the present Jerusalem. But the other woman corresponds to the Jerusalem above: she is free, and she is our mother." Philo's interpretation of the Torah was entitled "Allegories of the Law," and Origen (c.185–254 C.E.) made Christian allegory a major aspect of the interpretation of difficult passages.

Before the canon of the New Testament was agreed, there were many "apocryphal" writings ("things hidden away"), notably gospels aiming to fill in the gaps in the life and post-resurrection appearances of Jesus, including his descent into hell. These gospels also contained miraculous events, such as Jesus molding pigeons in clay, which then flew away. Letters and "acts" of apostles other than Paul and Peter often emphasized ascetic ideals, especially virginity. The *Acts of Thomas* is known complete in five languages and records his missionary work in India. Most of these apocrypha were excluded in the earliest NT canon, the Canon Muratori about 200 C.E. The fourteen or fifteen books of the Jewish apocrypha were not hidden or secret. They were included in the Septuagint, were largely accepted by Christians, and influenced the interpretation of the scriptures.

In the first two hundred years of the Church, the main emphases in writings and interpretations were on practical concerns, teaching new converts, many of whom were non-Jewish, and countering the growth of heretical ideas. In the next two hundred years different schools of thought developed, particularly in Alexandria around Origen with emphasis on the spiritual meaning of the soul's journey to God. The Church generally has been unable to accept Origen's ideas about soul, denying his belief that in a plurality of worlds there is transmigration of humans between them, but it was not until 553 C.E. that he was formally declared a heretic. The school in Antioch countered the allegorical approach of Alexandria, but the identification of heretics among them, such as Arius and Nestorius who speculated on the relation of the human and divine in Jesus, led to the suppression and loss of many of their writings. They defended the Bible as historical reality, especially the Genesis account of the Creation and the Fall, against the interpretations of exegetes in Alexandria.

Developments of Interpretation in the Western Church

The Western church, on the whole, stood aside from the arguments between the several schools of thought. They still admired Greek learning and recommended books from both Alexandria and Antioch, giving preference to Origen's spiritual exegesis. The apocalyptic book, the Revelation to John, was popular, but the expectation of an imminent end to the world was heavily criticized after about 200 C.E. According to Augustine, the scriptures give evidence of promise and fulfillment in the person of Jesus, and contain literally and figuratively answers to all the basic questions of humanity. He pleaded for competence in biblical languages and this came to be reflected in the teaching in the monasteries, and in their exegetical commentaries on whole books.

Jerome (342–420) aimed at producing Latin Christian literature to compare with that of the Romans, such as Virgil and Cicero. He provided new Latin translations of major parts of the Greek Septuagint. In 405 C.E., using established methods of classical exegesis based on the Hebrew, he produced a corrected version which included the New Testament and came to be known as the Latin Vulgate, *versio vulgata* (popular translation), the official scriptural text of the Roman Catholic Church. The Council of Trent (1545–63) authorized a revision of the several existing editions. A modern reworking, following the Second Vatican Council (1962–65), was largely completed in 1977. A Stuttgart edition (1994) has, in an appendix, the *Epistle to the Laodiceans* allegedly written by Paul. This invented letter aims to fill the apparent gap provided by Col. 4:16, "see that you read also the letter from Laodicea," implying that this is a letter written to Laodicea which was intended to be forwarded.

From the fifth century there was, in the West, emphasis on a fourfold pattern of exegesis—literal, allegorical, moral, and mystical. Anselm, born in Italy in 1033, Archbishop of Canterbury in 1093, where he died in 1109, has been called "The Father of Scholasticism." He rather overemphasized the ability of reason to lead to certain doctrines of revelation, and first used the expressions "faith seeking understanding" (*fides quaerens intellectum*) and "I believe, in order that I may understand" (*credo ut intelligam*), believing that the content of faith was rational. In the twelfth century there developed a resurgence of confidence after a period of limited scholarship. The emphasis turned to explanations of well-defined theological and doctrinal issues, on the basis of reason and recognized authority. Eastern and Arab scholars, such as Avicenna (980–1037) and Averrhoes (1126–98), preserved and translated into Arabic many works of Greek scholars, including Aristotle and Euclid. These had disappeared in Europe by the Middle Ages and might otherwise have been lost forever. Establishment of universities in the twelfth and thirteenth centuries came to be associated with this introduction of Aristotelian thought, and Thomas Aquinas (1225–74) claimed that truths of faith and truths of sense experience should be fully compatible and complementary. Believing that revelation is necessary to reach the truths of religion, he proceeded to make a synthesis of the Bible and Roman Catholic doctrine. There was diminishing regard for Aquinas until the end of the nineteenth century when a papal encyclical *Aeterni Patris* (1879) made Aquinas the basis for instruction in Roman Catholic schools. This was reaffirmed by another encyclical *Humani generis* in 1950, the first papal encyclical to permit belief in the evolutionary origins of the human body, but insisting on the special creation of Adam's soul. In 1992 Pope John Paul II, in a message to the Pontifical Academy of Sciences, said that "theories of evolution which consider the mind as emerging from the forces of living matter … are incompatible with the truth about man."

In the fifteenth century Renaissance humanists made important contributions to NT exegesis, rejecting scholastic theology and elaborate allegorical expositions. In the sixteenth century Erasmus and others produced critical editions of the Greek and Latin New Testaments. Their linguistic expertise contributed to the Reformation movements, with theologians of all persuasions seeking scriptural support for their views. In the same century, rebels against the Roman Catholic Church appealed to scripture, seeking to justify their defiance of the pope. Martin Luther (1483–1546) recognized and used

the Bible as his ultimate authority. Most of the major Protestant theologians followed his example. His vernacular translation, and the
advent of printing, greatly increased the reading of the scriptures by
the laity. Roman Catholic delegates at the Council of Trent (1545–63)
were encouraged to reform the education of clergy, and scholars
turned to using the Bible (in the Douai version, 1582–1609) as the
prime source to defend the Christian Fathers and Roman Catholic
doctrine. Inevitably the Bible became the basis of heated disputes
between different church communities, in which lay participation was
important. This led to violence and the Wars of Religion, with killing
of condemned heretics in the name of God.

BIBLICAL CRITICISM TODAY

The Bible is often referred to as "the word of God," but the words used
are in fact the words of human thought, and the most that ought to be
claimed is that they are inspired by God. The phrase used after Bible
readings is often "This is the word of the Lord." The phrase needs a
careful qualification in the mind of the hearer: "This *was* the word of
the Lord 2,000 years ago, to people of very different cultures." The
important realization is that so much is highly relevant today.

The interpretation must therefore be not only in terms of the words
used but also in the context of the believed time and place, when and
where they were first written. Insofar as time and place change for the
reader, so also one can expect the interpretation to change, not necessarily by a great deal, for it is remarkable and generally accepted that
the character and thoughts of humankind, their needs and fears, have
today much in common with those of people 2,000 years ago, in a variety of cultures. The actual changes can, nevertheless, sometimes be
quite important, for the language itself develops. Traditional beliefs
stemming from earlier biblical studies may then need to be revised, but
many texts contain timeless assurances that are readily committed to
memory. The available variety of translations of the Bible make the
committal to memory of individual verses much more difficult, unless
a favorite translation is adhered to.

Some denominations and church groups have identified doctrines that they declare cannot be changed, even though the doctrines are based on Bible passages written, translated, and interpreted many centuries ago. The writings belong to a different culture arising from less developed human knowledge and understanding, and before the increase of spiritual experience in a variety of patterns of worship and moral codes. The influences of science and linguistic analysis require careful attention, and space needs to be given to the implications of the saying of Jesus: "I still have many things to say to you, but you cannot bear them now. When the Spirit of truth comes, he will guide you into all the truth" (John 16:12–13). Most seekers for truth believe that the Spirit of truth has been active in earlier interpretations of the Bible and is still very active today.

The attempt to establish the "best" text is sometimes referred to as Lower Criticism. External criteria, such as manuscript variations, are linked to internal criteria such as the preference for the shorter of two versions of a phrase, in the belief that editors are likely to add a few words of explanation or correction.

Higher Criticism, developed in the eighteenth and nineteenth centuries, is concerned with such questions as Who wrote it? What sources were used? Were they reliable? What is the evidence of editing? Is there supporting historical evidence from other sources? When it was concluded by some that certain accounts were not literally true, many people were sufficiently disturbed to challenge the value of the activity. For those wishing to identify the reliability of evidence on which to base their beliefs, much can be learned from this Higher Criticism.

Linguistic Analysis emphasizes the importance of the meanings of words and idioms and the varieties of translations. An example of such analysis is given in relation to the "prediction" of the virgin birth of Jesus in Isa. 7:14, "Therefore the Lord himself will give you a sign. Look, the young woman is with child and shall bear a son, and shall name him Immanuel." In the Greek Septuagint, the Hebrew *almah* translated as "the young woman" is given as *parthenos,* which is commonly translated "virgin" but is also used by classical authors for "an unmarried woman who is not a virgin." This Greek word was the source of the use of this scripture by Matthew (1:23) with explicit reference to Mary and to Joseph. Similarly, in Luke 1:27, Mary is described as a virgin "engaged to Joseph," and when told that she would bear a son her response is "How can this be, since I am a virgin?" This is reinforced by Luke in 3:23, where he refers to Jesus as "the son (as was thought) of Joseph." Matthew (1:18–24) presents the story more from the point of view of Joseph who, when "she was found to be with child from the Holy Spirit," "planned to dismiss her quietly." The passage from Isaiah is again invoked, and Joseph takes Mary "as his wife." Apart from Matthew and Luke there is no reference to the virginal conception or virgin birth anywhere in the New Testament. The argument from silence, however, can never be final, as we shall see below, in relation to the attitude to unchastity.

As early as the second century, Jewish scholarship pointed out that the Hebrew word in the original language of Isaiah means simply "young woman," and, as a contemporary word of prophetic encouragement, may well have referred to an identifiable young woman, able to fulfill the prophecy for the people of that time, without any implication of miracle. The meaning in Isaiah of "Immanuel," namely "God with us," was found, however, to be doubly significant for Jesus. Miraculous birth stories are not unknown in the Bible, for example, Abraham and Sarah (Gen 17:15–19, 18:9–15, and 21:1–7), and were common in the Greek and Roman traditions. The Virgin Birth was a strongly held popular belief, accepted by the Church by the second century. The dogma of the Immaculate Conception, Mary without the taint of Original Sin, was made an official belief of the Roman Catholic Church in 1854.

Modern biblical criticism has to operate in the context of a number of difficult doctrines adhered to by some churches. The silences of scripture can often be important; thus Paul makes no reference to the Virgin Birth and the miracles of the Gospels, except for the Resurrection and Ascension. This may indicate that at least some of the miracles were not thought to be necessary parts of fundamental Christian belief.

An example of the problem of the absence of a key phrase in one

Gospel and its presence in another is afforded by Matt 5:31–32 where Jesus says, "It was also said, 'Whoever divorced his wife, let him give her a certificate of divorce.' But I say to you that anyone who divorces his wife, except on the ground of unchastity, causes her to commit adultery; and whoever marries a divorced woman commits adultery." A parallel saying is given in Matt 19:9, "whoever divorces his wife, except for unchastity, and marries another commits adultery." The parallel saying in Mark 10:11 (and likewise in Luke 16:18) omits "except for unchastity" and reads, "Whoever divorces his wife and marries another commits adultery against her," continuing significantly, "and if she divorces her husband and marries another, she commits adultery." The phrase "except for unchastity" is missing from some important manuscripts of Matthew's Gospel.

The meaning of the Matthew saying needs to be studied in the Jewish context. Hillel (60 B.C.E.–10 C.E.) allowed divorce "for any cause," but Shammai (c. 50 B.C.E.–c. 30 C.E.) supported "except for fornication." Does Jesus take sides? And what exactly is meant by "unchastity"? The law concerning a wife who commits adultery is given in Deut. 22:13ff. and prescribes stoning as the punishment. Why is this not mentioned here? Again Jewish law did not permit a wife to divorce her husband, whereas Greek and Roman law allowed this. According to Mark and Luke, it seems that Jesus treated men and women on the same basis, which is a remarkable variation of the traditional Jewish law. This is supported by Paul with a rare direct reference to a command of Jesus. He writes in 1 Cor. 7:10–11, some ten years or more before the Gospels were written, "To the married I give this command—not I but the Lord—that the wife should not separate from her husband (but if she does separate, let her remain unmarried or else be reconciled to her husband), and that the husband should not divorce his wife." This appears to be close to Mark and Luke and is consonant with the high standards set by Jesus, but is in conflict with Matthew's version of what Jesus said.

The authorship of books in both the Old and the New Testaments is a rich field of study, as part of Higher Criticism. Claims that the Pentateuch was written by Moses have long been discarded. Isaiah seems to have been written by at least three people living many years apart. The Psalms are often ascribed to David and that may be true for many of them. Psalm 3 has the title "A Psalm of David, when he fled from his son Absalom," and seventy-two other Psalms have titles referring to David. It was not unusual for a writer to use a name such as David to attempt to authenticate his work, but the test of time was the severest measure of the value of a Psalm. There is internal evidence of the Psalms being composed and collected over a period of some six hundred years. A similar situation occurs for the Song of Solomon, with little agreement on its authorship and its date, although the final form is thought to be from 450–400 B.C.E. There is no evidence for the attribution to Solomon other than that of tradition. No hint of the actual author or authors appears in the text.

The names linked to the Gospels as purported authors are not necessarily correct, and the relation between their texts reveals something of their interdependence and their dependence on other sources. Likewise some Epistles may not be by the traditionally assigned authors. The style of Hebrews is so different from letters accepted as written by Paul that it has long been agreed by most scholars that he did not write that book. Clement of Alexandria (c. 150–c. 215) questioned the Pauline authorship, and his pupil, Origen (185–254 C.E.) remarked, "Who wrote the Epistle, God only knows." In the same way, the book of the Revelation to John is different in style from both the Fourth Gospel and the Epistles assigned to John, so much so that the acceptance of Revelation into the canon was one of the last to be determined. Luther went further and rejected James, Hebrews, and Revelation.

Evidence of the development of theology in the Early Church can be found in many places in the New Testament. Two major examples are, first, the much-debated decision to accept non-Jews into the church with no restrictions, and, second, the inclusion of Hellenic ideas, notably so-called Gnostic teaching, from *gnosis*, the Greek word for "knowledge." The latter is, most probably, the basis of the warning in 1 Tim. 6:20–21: "Avoid the profane chatter and contradictions of what is falsely called knowledge, by professing it some have missed the mark as regards the faith." Although some scholars think Gnosticism is apparent in the mind of the author of the Fourth Gospel, there are really little more than traces of Gnosticism as a current heresy in the New Testament, and the characteristics of full-blown Gnosticism are absent. Thus there is no direct mention of the Gnostic belief in cosmic dualism, that is, the belief in a transcendent true God with a lesser God as the Creator God of the Bible. The Creator was referred to by Gnostics as the Demiurge, identified with evil in the Persian religion.

Form criticism pays special attention to literary units in the Gospels that have an identifiable form or function, for example, controversy with the Jews, pronouncements, or miracles, and units that appear to derive from oral tradition. Form criticism was distrusted by those who saw so-called redaction critics emphasize the tracing of the way traditions and their literature developed. These redaction critics looked for the results of editing and revision, possibly by an identifiable school, church, or community.

Historians, secular, Christian, and Jewish, have paid careful attention to some of the events of the Bible, in particular the birth of Jesus who is believed to have been born in 5 or 4 B.C.E. before the death of Herod in 4 B.C.E. (Matt. 2:19, Luke 1:5). The ancient traditional location is Bethlehem, as in Matt. 2:1–6, and Luke 2:1–4, but neither Mark nor John mentions Bethlehem. Luke's explanation is the decree from Emperor Augustus that all the world should be registered (Luke 2:1–4), for which there is no independent reliable record. The census of Quirinius, governor of Syria, was in 6 or 7 C.E., and Joseph alone could have registered without leaving Galilee. Matthew is clearly influenced by Micah 5:2 with its prediction that "a ruler" shall come from Bethlehem. If Bethlehem really was the family home of Joseph, surely there would have been a member able to provide a better cradle than a manger (Luke 2:7). Matt. 2:11 indicates that Jesus was born in a house. The birth of Jesus is more likely in Nazareth, as believed by the crowd who said, "Surely the Messiah does not come from Galilee… [but] from Bethlehem" (John 7:41–42). John does not deny Galilee or affirm Bethlehem.

The genealogies in Matt. 1:1–17 and Luke 3: 23–38 aim to show that

Jesus through Joseph was of Davidic descent, but they are very different. Luke has forty-one generations from David to the birth of Jesus,
and Matthew has only twenty-eight, with only three names common
to both. These genealogies cannot both be historical, and may be based
on unrecorded theological principles.

CHAPTER 5

Evidence Other Than in the Bible

THOSE WHO BELIEVE in a Creator God can reasonably expect that the nature of the Universe tells them something of what God is like. The discoveries of scientists then become evidence for the nature of God, and in the following three chapters and elsewhere I shall consider this evidence.

For people who are aware of spiritual or religious experiences, these become evidence relating to their beliefs. This evidence is considered in chapter 12 and the following chapters, and at various points in the discussion of evidence.

EVIDENCE FROM ARCHAEOLOGY

Archaeological evidence can be valuable in many ways. It can sometimes help to date events and identify the people involved, with their successes or failures in military conflict. It can identify religious practices and give some idea of the wealth and cultural standing of a people. There are often alternative interpretations, and in some cases we are not able to identify a really reliable piece of relevant information. We have already considered the absence of evidence from archaeology in relation to Solomon and David (see chapter 1).

A major problem in Egyptian and related archaeology is the establishment of an agreed chronology. For decades there has been an "Orthodox Chronology" (I prefer "Old Chronology" OC), now challenged by the "New Chronology" (NC), which for the earlier periods can be different by hundreds of years. Old Chronology relied mainly on the "Royal Canon" papyrus, now in the Turin Museum, which gives the order and period of each reign, for three hundred kings of Egypt, together with significant astronomical events. Another list of kings and events is provided by Manetho, a fourth-century B.C.E. Greek historian, quoted by Josephus in the first century C.E. The reliability of these lists is diminished by the omission of some kings, the inclusion of some otherwise unknown kings, the overlapping of reigns, variations due to latitude, and unrecorded adjustments of the calendar.

It is necessary to pin down the date of at least one astronomical event. The chosen event for the Old Chronology was the "heliacal rising" of Sirius, or Sothis, the brightest star in the sky, when the star arose just separated from the light of the sun. The Sothic date was a very special religious event when it coincided with the first day of the civil calendar. Such an occasion, reported by the Roman historian Censorinus, led to the issue of a coin by the Romans in 139 C.E. As the same event occurs every 1,460 years (= 4×365), it occurred in 1321 and 2781 B.C.E. The Sothic date is given in the Royal Canon for the seventh year of the reign of Senuseret III on the 226th day of the civil calendar.

The Egyptians used a "civil" calendar with 365 days in a year. There was also a "religious" calendar, based on celestial events, which follows a year of 365 ¼ days. This meant that over a period of 730 (= 2 × 365) years, midsummer occurred when the "date" was winter. A thirteenth-century B.C.E. papyrus reads "winter has come in summer." The calendars move out of coincidence by one day every four years, which is corrected by our use of "leap year," with February 29 added for every year divisible by four (for years that are multiples of 100, only those years exactly divisible by 400 are leap years). This produces an average length of year of 365.24250 days compared with the most accurate measured length of 365.24220 days. To be out by 226 days implies a period of 4 × 226 = 904 years, so the seventh year of Senuseret III must have been in 2781 × 904 = 1877 B.C.E., using only the date of the Roman coin, 4 × 226 years, and the Royal Canon record. The New Chronology dates Senuseret III 1698–1660 B.C.E. The conflict of evidence is used to cast doubt on Sothic dating.

The New Chronology pays special attention to astronomical events, including eclipses of the moon and the sun, carefully recorded as "omens," and lunar month-lengths. From hundreds of recorded events it is possible to use a computer to retrocalculate (i.e., calculate backwards in time) such events and to check their dates against a proposed chronology. This is a huge, ongoing study, but already there are some convincing and impressive successes. For example, from lunar month-length data from papyri, as many as thirty-seven out of thirty-nine events in a given period of New Chronology years, 1694–1644 B.C.E., have been found to agree. The other two events could have suffered from limited viewing conditions. This is to be compared with only twenty-one events agreeing in the same period, considered in the Old Chronology to span 1832–1781 B.C.E. The New Chronology dates take careful note of OT evidence and make Moses (1530–1406 B.C.E.) a near contemporary of the Law Giver Hammurabi (1565–1523 B.C.E.), whereas the OC dates put Hammurabi several centuries before Moses. With the New Chronology it is easier to believe that Moses was influenced by Hammurabi. The difficult-to-believe life spans of the Patriarchs, for example, 969 years for Methuselah, are interpreted as the duration not of a single person but of a family of several or many closely related members. The sojourn in Egypt is given as 430 years in Exod. 12:40–41 using the Massoretic Hebrew text. The Greek text of the Septuagint reads this as the period of sojourn in both Egypt and Canaan, allowing the period in Egypt to be brought down to about 215 years.

Jacob (= Israel) and his family were in Egypt in the eighteenth century B.C.E. (OC), or seventeenth (NC). Jacob's family may be one of the Hyksos tribes, a Greek name for "desert princes." References to the Hyksos in Egyptian records show that they soon outnumbered the local population, with their center at Avaris, in Goshen, in the northeast of the delta region. This is where the Israelites are told to settle (Gen. 45:10). The Israelites, possibly known as Hebrews before the Exodus, about 1447 B.C.E. (NC) or 1360 (OC), are now often identified with the inscriptions "Habiru" and "Hapiru," or "apiru." Some 3,600 are reported as doing hard labor. Even after the Exodus other Habiru were making bricks, implying that not all the Hebrews escaped from Egypt.

There are so many contributions of archaeology that relate to biblical accounts surrounding the Exodus, some of them conflicting, that it is difficult to know which ones to select. One such topic is so far from agreement that I shall leave it out. That is the identity of Moses and his role in the story of the Israelites. Mose, with a divine or other prefix, was a common name.

Another undecided topic is the route of the Exodus. One suggestion is that the crossing was near the midpoint of the Gulf of Aqaba, the right arm of the Red Sea, where the water is relatively shallow. Underwater archaeology has revealed coral-encrusted remains of chariot wheels at each end of the proposed crossing. Others suggest a crossing into Sinai at a point east of Avaris with a route to the east of the Gulf of Suez. In both cases, miraculous winds and earthquakes are involved.

The date of the Exodus can be deduced from 1 Kings 6:1, which says that Solomon began to build his temple 480 years after the Exodus. By the times of the reign of Solomon, Old Chronology and New Chronology have come into close agreement, 965–926 (OC) and 971–931 (NC), making the Exodus 1447 (NC) and 1441 (OC). The 480 years agrees approximately with total years, symbolic and rounded, after Deut. 1:3, but some scholars question its validity.

An intriguing and related topic is the eruption of the volcano Thera, which produced the island of Santorini, north of Crete, with its bay measuring ten kilometers in diameter. One theory notes that the initial *tsunami* or tidal wave produced by the eruption could have been tens of meters high, reaching the Egyptian coast, five hundred miles to the south, within an hour, and one of a series of subsequent waves, arriving two days later, could be more than two meters high. There it would have raised the sea level near the narrow strip of reed covered land between "Lake" Manzala, north of Avaris, and the sea. At first the sea would have withdrawn, returning about two hours later. One dating of the Thera event depends on cores of ice from Greenland, obtained in 1980, showing year-by-year strata. The layer for the Pompeii eruption in 79 C.E. had high levels of acidity. A similar result occurred for 1390 B.C.E., plus or minus fifty years, which could be due to the eruption of Thera.

Several investigators of the plagues have suggested that they could be explained as normal physical and biological events, such as those encountered with recent volcanic eruptions. The result of Thera's explosion (Exod. 7:12–10:23) could have been darkness in Egypt for three days, thunder and hail and fire, dust killing all the cattle, fish dying and turning rivers red ("blood"), lice, flies, and locusts, and also frogs. It is clear, however, that the sequence of natural explanations does not agree with the biblical sequence of events. The protection of the Israelites is also not explained, nor the deaths of the first-born of the Egyptians (Exod. 11:5). One suggestion is that the Egyptians killed their own first-born to provide an impressive placation of the perceived anger of their gods, a practice known at that time and present even in the Bible—2 Kings 3:27, Judg. 11:30, Jer. 7:30–31.

There seems to be a major timing flaw in attributing to the eruption of Thera both the plagues and the crossing of the Red Sea. It would take about two days for the Israelites, alerted by darkness over the land, to march from their center at Avaris to the coast of "Lake" Manzala, by which time one of the *tsunami* waves could conveniently arrive. But the hatching of frogs and other biological events would take much longer than two days, and allowing for the effects of the plagues to develop before the Israelites were released by Pharaoh, this would mean that the *tsunami* events would have largely died out. The attractions of using Thera for dating the Exodus are open to question.

On the other hand, the dating of the Exodus about 1360 B.C.E. (OC), when Thera erupted, fits well with radiocarbon dating, made in 1996, of the fall of Jericho. Dates from cereal grains excavated in the 1950s range from 1397–1244 B.C.E., with an average of 1320 B.C.E. This fits with the Bible account of forty years wandering in the wilderness (Josh. 5:6), but conflicts with the New Chronology dating.

The date of 1360 B.C.E. (OC) for the Exodus also relates to the reign of the pharaoh Akhenaten, 1350–1334 B.C.E. (OC), son of Amonhotep III, husband of the celebrated beauty Nefertiti. Akhenaten was the first historical figure to establish a state religion based on monotheism—the cult of the Aten, the sun god or solar disc, first mentioned in Egypt around 1450 B.C.E. (OC). This pharaoh fought the state religion of Amon, moved the capital from Thebes to Amarna, and tried to obliterate all traces of the polytheism of his ancestors. By his people,

Akhenaten was considered to be a god, but he never called himself "god," referring to himself as "Son of God." It has been suggested that the religion of the Hebrews impressed the Egyptians and this led to monotheistic Atenism becoming dominant after the experiences of the Exodus. However, the New Chronology date of 1447 B.C.E. for the Exodus is a long time before the New Chronology date for Akhenaten, 1023–1007. Akhenaten's younger brother, Tutankhamun, who succeeded him, moved the capital back to Thebes and reestablished polytheism.

Evidence from archaeology is still accumulating, with serious conflicts between the Old and New Chronology. Scientific datings from astronomical retrocalculations, Greenland ice cores, and radiocarbon dating need to be properly correlated. Many discovered inscriptions confirm details of the OT accounts, but some are open to challenge. Hasty conclusions are unwise.

Expressions of Christian Belief in Hymns

As might be expected, most of the expressions of belief in Christian hymns, songs, and choruses derive from the Bible, explicitly or implicitly. These expressions are evidence of the beliefs of the authors, and they influence the beliefs of those who sing the hymns. To that extent, they are evidence that acts as bases for belief or for reinforcement or changing of existing beliefs. It is debatable how literally the images are interpreted today since it is easy to be carried away more by the music and poetry than by the meanings implied. Hymns are readily committed to memory and are more frequently, and more accurately, recalled than verses in the Bible, especially now that there are so many different versions of the Bible text. Hymns often form a larger part of worship than Bible readings, and may therefore be more influential.

In relation to chapter 16 (on Incarnation and Atonement), I felt it was worth reading through three hymnbooks in order to analyze the frequencies of occurrence of references to different images of the Atonement. The first book selected was *Hymns Ancient and Modern New Standard* (AMNS), first published in 1983, containing 333 hymns

(1–333) derived from *Ancient and Modern Revised* (AMR, 1950), with one hundred added (334–433) from *100 Hymns for Today* (1969) and a further one hundred (434–533) from *More Hymns for Today* (1980). The second hymnbook chosen was *Common Praise* (CP), published in 2000, with 628 hymns. The third hymnbook was *Mission Praise* (MP), published in 1990 with a total of 798 hymns, songs, and choruses. Of these, about 560 are typical hymns, and many of the 238 songs and choruses use repeated phrases to provide greater emphases. In the counting of frequencies of key words, multiple occurrences are counted as two, even when many more occur in one hymn. "Adam" occurs sixteen times in AMNS no. 369, and "Savior" occurs sixteen times in MP no. 672. See pp. 133–135 for details of the analyses for Atonement.

EVIDENCE FROM THE ARTS

Evidence provided by the arts is in many ways close to the evidence from spiritual experience. By "the arts" we mean not only painting, sculpture, architecture, music, singing, and dance, but also literature, poetry, the theatre, and the writing of history. This is a large subject deserving a special study. Perhaps there is an author, more skilled than I, who could write on something like "Evidence from the Arts as a Basis for Christian Belief." This would be very different from the evidence from the sciences since it would be received in a wide variety of ways by people from different cultures, and by people of different ages in a given culture, and at different times in history.

Experience of the arts falls mainly into two categories: the realm of nature and the realm of human creativity. The former will parallel scientists' discovery of the order in Creation, with a key element identified as beauty. Scientists assign importance to beauty in their mathematical theories and models. Streamlining is aerodynamically efficient; it is also beautiful. Immediately we see one of the difficulties in this subject. Whereas almost all humans would accept that there is great importance in beauty, not all would agree what is beautiful. Beauty in nature is more likely to be universally recognized than the beauty in the created works of humans. This is nowhere more appar-

EVIDENCE OTHER THAN IN THE BIBLE 57

ent than in present-day painting, sculpture, and music. Yet many religious people find inspiration in these same fields, including a sense of awe and mystery, and means to express human experience that fails to find its outlet in language.

Literature, poetry, the theatre, and the writing of history have a different approach to creativity since they depend on words, and in the case of theatre (and opera and choirs) these engage with the physical performance of people. These arts allow a more ready identification of the reader or observer with an explicit human experience, and invite discussion and evaluation in the same terms. They reveal other qualities in addition to beauty, especially the truths that they convey concerning the thoughts and beliefs of humans. Now we are closer to seeing the importance of evidence from these forms of the arts in forming the basis for Christian belief. The quality of literature in the writing of history, or in the presentation of beliefs, can be important in conveying that relevant evidence. The quality can reflect the seriousness of reliance on that evidence, and its transparency can lead to an easier appreciation of the points being made.

Poetry has a special place among the arts. Wordsworth wrote, "[P]oetry takes its origin from emotion recollected in tranquillity," and both emotion and tranquility can be important in considering the bases of our beliefs. Some words are instinctive, others chosen, juxtaposed with startling originality and surprising effect, inviting new associations of ideas and attention to the music of the writing. Poetry is not always easy to follow, nor is it free from ambiguity and even obscurity. As such, it is sometimes more evident of the need to consider available evidence of other kinds rather than as evidence in itself.

WRITINGS IN THE FIRST AND SECOND CENTURIES

Christian

The *Didache*, or *Teaching of the 12 Apostles (to the Gentiles)*, is an eleventh-century manuscript, rediscovered in 1873, and believed to have been compiled in the second century. A fourth-century Greek fragment shows that it was known in Egypt at that time. Its food regulations and table prayers, and the section titled "Two Ways—Life and Death," link it to a strongly Jewish community, with parallels in Qumran material. It contains a section on morals followed by one on church discipline, including, "Let your fasts not coincide with those of the hypocrites. They [Pharisees] fast on Monday and Thursday, you, though, should fast on Wednesday and Friday." Baptism is, ideally, by total immersion. The Lord's prayer reads, "Give us today our bread for the morrow." There are two eucharistic prayers, with the cup before the loaf, and the repeated "To you be glory forever," but there is no mention of "body" or "blood." Strangely, in sections referring to bishops and deacons, there is no mention of presbyters (= priests). However, apostles, prophets, and teachers are mentioned.

The *Epistle of Barnabas* has much in parallel with the Didache. Dated early second century, it aims to reclaim Jewish Christians tempted to return to Judaism. Authorship is unknown, but it is quoted by Clement of Alexandria (150–215 C.E.) as "scripture," and by Origen (185–254 C.E.) as a Catholic Epistle.

The *Letters of Ignatius* were probably written on the way to his martyrdom in Rome in 107 C.E. Their main concern is defense of an authoritarian episcopacy and against a Judaizing heresy.

Non-Christian

Josephus (37–c. 100 C.E.) was a Jew with pro-Roman sympathies, a priest, soldier, and historian. He wrote many books (29?) including the famous *Jewish Antiquities*, the history of the Jews from the earliest times up to the end of the reign of Nero. He refers briefly to the martyrdom of James in 62 C.E., "the brother of Jesus called the Messiah," and adds more about Jesus.

> About this time there lived Jesus, a wise man, (if indeed one ought to call him a man). For he was one who wrought surprising feats and was a teacher of such people as accept the truth gladly. He won over many Jews and many of the Greeks. (He was the Messiah.) When Pilate, upon hearing him accused by men of the highest standing amongst us, had

condemned him to be crucified, those who had in the first place come to love him did not give up their affection for him. (On the third day he appeared to them restored to life, for the prophets of God had prophesied these and countless other marvelous things about him.) And the tribe of Christians, so called after him, has still to this day not disappeared.

The sentences in parentheses are believed by many modern scholars to have been interpolated by Christian scribes.

The Roman historian Tacitus (c. 55–117 C.E.) records how Nero blamed the Christians for the great fire of Rome in 64 C.E., which many thought Nero himself started. Tacitus records how Nero inflicted "the most elaborate punishments upon those people, hated for their crimes, who were commonly styled "Christians."

> Their founder, Christus, had been executed in the reign of Tiberius (14–37 C.E.) by Pontius Pilate, governor of Judaea. But despite this temporary setback the pernicious superstition had broken out anew, not only in Judaea, where the trouble had started, but even in Rome where all things horrible or shameful in the world collect and find a vogue. First, Nero had Christians who confessed their faith arrested. Then, on their information, large numbers of others were condemned —not so much for incendiarism as because they were hated by the human race. . . . They were torn to pieces by dogs, or crucified, or made into torches to be lit after dark as substitutes for daylight. . . . Despite their guilt as Christians, and the ruthless punishment it deserved, the victims were pitied. For it was thought that they were being sacrificed to one man's brutality rather than to the national interest.

Both Peter and Paul apparently suffered martyrdom in these persecutions.

Suetonius, another Roman historian (c. 70–130 C.E.), in his biography of the emperor Claudius (ruled 41–54 C.E.), mentions Christians as troublemakers. He notes the expulsion from Rome in 49 C.E., of "the Jews who under the influence of Chrestus [i.e., Christus, or Christ] were constantly causing disturbances." This was only sixteen years after the death of Jesus, and some prefer the report in Acts 18:2 that "Claudius had ordered all Jews to leave Rome." Suetonius also reported on the incidents under Nero: "punishment was inflicted on the Christians, a class of men given to a new and mischievous superstition."

Pliny the Younger (c. 61–112 C.E.), a scholar of repute, was a friend of Tacitus and governor of the province of Bithynia-Pontus in Asia Minor. He wrote a long letter to the emperor Trajan asking for advice on how to conduct the trials of Christians. For example, was the simple confession "I am a Christian" a crime? Pliny stated that Christianity was widespread, attracted a great number of all ages and ranks, and affected country districts as well as towns. The temples of the gods had been deserted, and the market for fodder for the sacrificial animals had fallen very low. Pliny reported that Christians "claimed that their only fault or mistake was their custom of meeting regularly before daybreak to sing a hymn in alternate verses to Christ as if to a God and to promise with an oath [*sacramentum*] . . . not to commit a theft, fraud or adultery, break their word, or deny a trust when summoned to hand it over." The word *sacramentum* probably had a deeper meaning for the Christians and referred to the "mystery" of the Eucharist. The reply from Trajan recommended tolerance, with no fixed rules, yet leaving Christianity as a crime deserving punishment. Pliny was able to avoid persecuting Christians but under Trajan (53?–117) Ignatius, Bishop of Antioch, suffered martyrdom.

These examples of non-Christian writings give ample evidence of the existence of Jesus, refuting the denials of some critics of Christianity. They tell us more—that Jesus was well known for his teaching and miracles, and that he suffered a violent death. It is also clear that early Christians were sufficiently confident of the evidence for their faith that they chose martyrdom rather than deny their Savior.

CHAPTER 6

Physical Evolution

SCIENTISTS INVESTIGATE the universe, and those pre-pared to be convinced of the necessity of a divine Cre-ator are endeavoring to discover the nature of God's creation. Its nature tells us something about its Creator, and the principal charac-teristics appear to be the predominance and necessity of order, the uni-versal process of evolution, and the remarkable potential for the evolution and continuity of humankind.

ASTRONOMY

Observations of the movements of the planets over many centuries finally led to the realization that the earth is in orbit about the sun. The first suggestion of a heliocentric solar system was made by Aristarchus of Samos in the period 280–264 B.C.E., following similar hypotheses of Pythagoras (582?–500 B.C.E.) and his followers. Aristarchus believed that the earth and the other planets orbited the sun, and con-cluded that the earth also rotates on its axis once in twenty-four hours. However, the dominance of Aristotelian thought led to the rejection of heliocentricity and the acceptance of the geocentric system of Ptolemy of Alexandria (100–170? C.E.). The explanation of the fact that the sun appears to orbit about the earth, rising in the east and set-ting in the west, is that the earth rotates from west to east on its axis once in twenty-four hours. Aquinas (1225–74) considered this a pos-sibility. The geocentric theory requires the sun and the whole of the star system to rotate about the earth once in twenty-four hours.

Heliocentricity was not supported with satisfactory evidence until the time of Copernicus (1473–1543 C.E.). He did not carry out exper-iments but thought out an explanation of the known relationships in the solar system that was more convincing and elegant than the Ptolemaic picture of the earth as the central object in the universe. His heliocentric beliefs were essentially completed in 1510, but he still recognized problems, such as the fact that the movement of the earth about the sun should result in an apparent motion in the stars, known as parallax. This was later realized to be a much smaller effect than originally expected because the stars were far beyond the planets. Parallax was first observed by Bessel in 1838.

Copernicus's caution, based in part on known theological objections, prevented his book *On the Revolution of the Celestial Spheres* from being published before his death in 1543. The book's unsigned preface, written by Osiander, stated that the theory was simply a calculational device with no relation to reality, which served to avoid theological difficulties but did not represent the beliefs of Copernicus. Theological objections included reference to Bible passages believed to support the geocentric theory, for example, Josh. 10:12–13: "Sun, stand still at Gibeon, and Moon in the valley of Aijalon. And the sun stood still, and the moon stopped, until the nations took vengeance on their enemies. . . . The sun stopped in mid-heaven, and did not hurry to set for about a whole day." Several references to sunrise and sunset were also included (Ps. 19:6; Sir. = Ecclesiasticus 1:5 and 26:16; Job 9:7). The book was put on the index of prohibited books in 1616, the year in which Galileo was told by Pope Paul V not to "hold, defend, or teach" his heliocentric beliefs, and it remained on the index until 1835.

The tardiness of this revision of Christian belief arose from two main considerations. The first was the belief that the importance of humankind meant that humanity's dwelling place would be the center of the universe. The other was the continuing dominance of Aristotle's (384–322 B.C.E.) philosophy in the works of Thomas Aquinas (1225–1274 C.E.) whose metaphysics, believed by some to have held up the advance of empirical science, was accepted by the Church at that time.

Conflict between the Church authorities and scientists who were convinced that heliocentricity was the best available theory continued during Galileo's lifetime (1564–1642). He was, in many respects, one of the first productive scientists, in the modern sense of scientist, relying on observations, and propounding theories that could be disproved by observation. His improved design of contemporary telescopes in 1609 led to the discovery of four satellites of Jupiter, as recorded in his influential book The Starry Messenger. A little later he observed the phases of Venus, which prove that Venus orbits the sun. In 1616 Pope Paul V appointed consulters to study the issue and they found against Galileo. He continued to write about scientific method, notably his book The Assayer in 1623, and The Dialogue in 1632. The Inquisition in 1633 required him to say, "I abjure, curse and detest my errors," and he was sentenced to life imprisonment, which was later reduced to house arrest. He died in 1642.

As late as the Second Vatican Council (1962–65) it was noted that in the past some Christians "did not show themselves sufficiently aware of the legitimate autonomy of science." Pope John Paul II (1920–2005) admitted that Galileo "had much to suffer." He set up a Commission in 1982 to "deepen their study of the Galileo case and . . . to remove the barriers to a fruitful relation of science and faith that the Galileo affair still raises in many minds." Its findings and those of other studies were accepted at an official ceremony in 1992. The pope noted that the theologians of the Inquisition failed to re-examine their criteria of scriptural interpretation in the context of "the new science."

The Church has realized that it ought not to set up a committee to judge a purely scientific question. Remarks made by Pope Pius XII (1876–1958) appear to suggest that he has accepted that the Big Bang (p. 65) is a "proven" account of Creation. Those may well have been unwise and incautious remarks.

Copernicus and Galileo thought planet orbits were circles. Kepler (1571–1630) found that they were not circles but ellipses. Newton in 1684 discovered the law of gravity and showed that both circles and ellipses were possible.

Some people, having accepted that the earth orbits the sun, not surprisingly believe that the sun is the center of the universe. It is now established that the sun is far from the center of the Milky Way galaxy, and the position of the Milky Way galaxy in the universe is not known.

COSMOLOGY

The Milky Way is a galaxy of stars, in number several 100,000 million. Hubble in 1926 was the first to identify galaxies outside our galaxy and there is now evidence from the Hubble Space Telescope, established in 1993, of many million such extragalactic galaxies. The farthest are some 12,000 million light-years away—our sun is seven light-minutes away, at 93 million miles. The methods for determining distances are not easy to convey in a few words, but are accepted by nearly all scientists. Hubble was also the first, in 1929, to measure the velocity of recession of extragalactic galaxies. The velocity is measured by observing the frequencies of light, that is, the colors, emitted or absorbed by known chemical elements in the galaxies and noting the differences from the frequencies for the same elements on earth. This so-called Doppler effect has a parallel in the change of frequency of sound for objects moving toward or away from the listener. A commonly noticed example is for a motorcycle, which appears to emit a higher note on approaching and a lower note on receding from a listener. Hubble found that the velocities of galaxies' recession were proportional to their distances from us, and the constant of proportionality is now known as the Hubble constant. At first this might seem to indicate that the earth is indeed the center of the universe, but by drawing a two-dimensional map of distributed galaxies, each with an arrow of length and direction indicating its velocity as viewed from the earth, it is fairly easy to see that each and every galaxy finds that all the other galaxies appear to recede from it at velocities proportional to their distance from it. This, in three dimensions, is an important characteristic of the universe and finds a natural explanation in Einstein's general theory of relativity formulated in 1915 and published in 1916.

As early as 1922, the Russian physicist and mathematician Friedman had solved Einstein's equations for the universe and he showed that they led to an expanding universe, a result obtained independently by the Belgian Abbé Lemaitre. Einstein was not happy with this result because he believed the universe was essentially constant in size. He introduced an arbitrary constant into his equations, known as the Cosmological Constant, to yield a static solution to general relativity. Later, when Hubble's evidence of the expansion of the universe was accepted, Einstein removed the constant, and later declared it to be the biggest error he ever made. Recently an observation with the Hubble Telescope indicated that the most distant galaxies appear to be receding more rapidly than would be expected when allowance is made for the gravitational pull of the rest of the universe. It has been suggested that the reintroduction of a modified cosmological constant could account for this. This is a typical example of improvement in both observations and theories, and the implications may lead to a change of hitherto fundamental beliefs. Some revision of the details of the history of the early universe would then be required, while retaining the overall picture of an expanding universe.

PHYSICS

Once it is accepted that the universe is expanding, it is obvious that, looking back in time, the universe was once smaller. In the ultimate backward look, some 12,000 million years ago, the universe occupied an extremely small spherical region. The known laws of physics require its temperature to have been unimaginably large. So in the beginning of creation a point-like object immediately expanded in what has become known as the Big Bang. This name was first suggested by Fred Hoyle in 1950, one of the opponents of the theory, to make it sound ludicrous. It is peculiarly inappropriate because for some time after the beginning of creation there was no possibility of sound. One of the consequences of Einstein's theory is that space and time are linked, time being treated as a fourth dimension with the three dimensions of space. There was no time before creation. The expansion was not into existing space; it made its space and time as it expanded. The creation of the universe was not in time, but rather time began with creation, as first proposed and argued by St. Augustine (354–430): "There is no time before the world began" because "without motion and change there is no time."

The evidence for the evolution of the physical universe, leading to the formation of atoms, stars, and galaxies, can be found in known physical laws. The Big Bang was associated with intense, high-energy, electromagnetic radiation. As the expansion took place, the universe cooled down, and this radiation cooled down with it, from high energy x-rays to ultraviolet and visible light, and infrared and microwaves. Today, about 12,000 million years after the Big Bang, these shortwave radio waves, first detected in 1965 by Penzias and Wilson, can be studied. They have all the expected characteristics, such as intensity as a function of wavelength, with minute fluctuations as evidence of the formation of galaxies. Further confirmation of the Big Bang is found in explanations of the chemical composition of matter in the universe, based on well-known nuclear processes. The picture is remarkably detailed and some features remain to be agreed. Exotic supplementary and alternative theories are being explored, but the evolution of the physical universe is now generally accepted by nearly all scientists and is most unlikely to be overthrown as science progresses.

In the context of this persuasive evidence it is possible to think through Christian beliefs. A key question is "What caused the Big Bang?" The principal alternative answers appear to be God, sheer chance, or both. Strangely enough, the next problem is not "Where did all the energy and matter come from?" because modern physics shows that it can arise spontaneously from nothing. It is interesting to note that creation *ex nihilo*, in some sense, was one of Aquinas's beliefs in the thirteenth century.

The Anthropic Principle

A more searching question is "Where did the laws of physics come from, and how do the fundamental constants of physics, such as the strength of the force of gravity and the masses of the electron, proton and neutron, come about?" The deep significance of this question arises from the fact that if extremely small changes are made in almost any of the strengths of forces used in physics theories, the consequences are devastating. The main processes of physical evolution, such as star formation, the origin of the chemical elements and in particular carbon, and the nuclear processes that make stars like the sun radiate heat, all depend on the precise values of the physical constants that are measured by observation and used in physics theories. These processes are the bases for the emergence of life and the biological evolution leading to sentient and intelligent life forms. The universe seems to be made in such a precise way that humans can evolve, suggesting that creation is dependent on an anthropic (human-making) principle. This is a very different way of thinking from the barren belief in pure purposeless chance.

It would be unscientific to view this situation as a knockdown argument for the existence of a creator aiming to create humans. It is possible that more advanced physics theories will include reasons for the magnitudes of physical constants, or at least relationships between them. There may also be alternative ways of viewing the extraordinarily precise values needed for the constants to enable humans to evolve.

One such alternative approach is to speculate about the creation of multiple universes, even an infinite number. The argument can then be that all evolved in their own peculiar ways, determined by their values for the physical constants, and that we regard ourselves as a unique evolution because we are here to observe our universe. There are no known ways of communicating with those other universes, if they exist, so this hypothesis is unable to be tested or disproved, meaning it is not the usual sort of scientific hypothesis. It also flies in the face of the principle of "Ockham's razor"—"do not multiply hypotheses unnecessarily," a principle first found in Aristotle. William of Ockham (c. 1300–c. 1349), a Franciscan priest-philosopher, first applied the principle against the excesses of theologians in multiplying kinds of entity. The Anthropic Principle, like so many arguments relating to the existence and characteristics of God, is most convincing to those who already believe. This is quite close to Anselm's "I believe in order to understand" (*credo ut intelligam*). It is also close to the argument from design, which has had a checkered history, not least in relation to the theory of evolution.

CHAPTER 7

Geological Evolution

INTRODUCTION

As stated in chapter 6, we will not to go into details of the primary evidence leading to the theory of the Big Bang, and subsequent physical evolution, mainly because such detailed evidence would be very difficult to follow without a great deal of scientific study. In the same way we shall not go into details of geological evidence, except for one particular approach to the age of the earth, using radioactivity, which is overwhelmingly convincing. Two appendices are provided for readers who wish to study more closely the scientific evidence (pp. 181–84).

My primary concern is with evidence that acts as a basis for Christian belief, and all that is really needed are the agreed conclusions from geological research, and in particular those that are most unlikely to be seriously challenged by new discoveries or existing counterarguments. We noted above that some Christians hold beliefs that are not a recognizable part of specifically Christian beliefs, but stem from evidence that may have religious implications. For example, one well-known preacher teaches that, before the Fall, there was a "perfect" world, with no volcanoes or earthquakes to cause suffering to human beings. He believes that the after-effects of the sin of Adam invaded the whole of Creation. This flatly contradicts geological evidence. Belief in evolution gives quite different answers to these problems, but leaves the central question unanswered: "Why did God create a world with suffering and death?" In chapter 15, it is suggested that the good produced by the order in the universe outweighs the suffering that is caused by order.

Such problems are encountered in relation to "the age of the earth," which is not a part of specific Christian belief. Among Christians there are two quite different beliefs about the age of the earth; one follows closely the ages in years of people mentioned in the Bible, usually referred to as the "young earth theory," leading to an earth that would be some 6,000 years old, and the other is based on a variety of scientific measurements and estimates that arrive at the age of about 4,600 million years.

AGE OF THE EARTH

The solar system is believed by scientists to have formed from the debris of an exploding star, a supernova, the gases at the center forming the sun (a star), and the planets being formed from the surrounding dust. The supernovae occurred when the first generation of stars became exhausted by their radiance, between 7,000 and 8,000 million years after the Big Bang, having already produced all the natural chemical elements by nuclear reactions at extremely high star temperatures. When supernovae exploded, they scattered all the known elements into space, which then produced a second generation of stars and also planets and satellites like the earth and our moon. The age of the sun and the earth deduced from cosmology and physics, and confirmed by geology, is between 4,000 and 5,000 million years.

The time since Creation was estimated by Archbishop Ussher (1581–1656) from the Bible ages of generations since Adam. His famous answer for the date of Creation was 4004 B.C.E., that is, four millennia before the birth of Jesus in 4 B.C.E. Earlier estimates allowed six millennia from the Creation to the end of the world, corresponding to the six days of Creation. Each day was seen to be equivalent to 1,000 years from Ps. 90:4: "a thousand years in your sight are like yesterday." Two millennia were allowed for the period from the birth of Jesus to the end of the world. As 1994 C.E. (and 2000 C.E.) passed without the end of the world, the fear engendered by such predictions largely evaporated.

In 1654 Dr. John Lightfoot (1602–75) set the date of Creation at the September equinox, and later made it match the start of the academic year at Cambridge, where he was vice-chancellor. This placed creation on October 23, 4004 B.C.E., precisely at "the sensible hour of 9 a.m." This period has been interpreted by biblical literalists as the time since humans were first known, but originally it was believed that the creation of the universe, including the earth, and the creation of humans, took place at the same time, or very nearly so. Some adherents to the Bible account accept the evolution of the bodies of Homo sapiens, intelligent humans, and therefore also the earth, over a long period, but believe in the special creation of a human by adding a soul, making humankind in "the image and likeness of God." The transformation at a particular point in time, linked by some to 4004 B.C.E., is variously believed to have been in the "first" man, Adam, or simultaneously in the whole race or species of Homo sapiens. This is, of course, speculation, and no reason seems to be given, other than respect for the literal account in Genesis, for not accepting the process of evolution. An alternative belief is that members of Homo sapiens continued to evolve in their brains, and therefore in their mental activity, often equated with the development of their minds, and eventually experienced spiritual activity, often equated with the development of souls. Many would believe that humans are still evolving in a limited way physically, and their knowledge, understanding, and religious beliefs are still developing.

As early as 1830, the geologist Lyell and others realized that the formation of rocks by sedimentation required a very long interval of time, 75,000 years or more. Lord Kelvin, from a consideration of the time for the earth to cool to its present temperature, concluded that the age of the earth was between 20 and 400 million years and settled for 98 million years. However, he did not realize the importance of the heating effect of the radioactivity in the earth, nearly all of which is provided by the radioactive isotope Potassium-40. Today geologists generally agree that the earth is about 4,600 million years old.

The most convincing piece of evidence for the age of the rocks of the earth is provided by their radioactivity. The nuclei of radioactive atoms decay to stable or radioactive "daughter" nuclei of different chemical elements, either by the emission of nuclear particles, alphas (helium nuclei of mass 4) or betas (negative electrons) or positrons (positive electrons), or, for certain nuclei, by the capture of inner-shell atomic electrons. Another mode of decay, relatively very rare, found only for heavy nuclei such as uranium and thorium, is spontaneous fission into two roughly equal mass nuclei.

The half-life of a radioactive nucleus, which can be measured with considerable accuracy, is the time taken on average for half of a given number of nuclei of the parent to decay. Half-lives range from less than a millionth of a second to many millions of millions of years, and some nuclei are stable, that is, have an infinite half-life. A knowledge of the original abundance of the radioactive parent in a specimen and the present-day abundance, together with the value of the half-life, enables the specimen's age to be determined. An example of this is "radiocarbon" dating of dead organic material such as wood, seeds or fibers in material, with ages less than about 50,000 years (see Appendix A). Another method is available if the radioactive element in a rock decays to a stable daughter, as for Rubidium-87 decaying to Strontium-87, and that daughter can be assumed to have been absent when the rock was formed. A measurement of the ratio of the abundance of the stable daughter to that of the radioactive parent allows calculation of the age of the rock (see Appendix B). An example of each method is given.

Many more methods can provide estimates of the ages of rocks. Several radioactive isotopes, including Thorium-232, half-life 14.01 thousand million years, and Uranium-235, half-life 704 million years, are used to obtain independent ages for rocks, by comparisons of the measured abundances of members of the chains of daughter elements. These abundances can be measured by precision mass-spectrometers and other techniques. A major assumption is that the rock does not suffer losses of daughters by leaching or the escape of the gas radon, or suffers increases by contamination. Ages obtained from a variety of isotopic ratios detect any such errors and, if they are minimal, allow the ages of the rocks to be confidently measured.

On the basis of a number of reasonable assumptions, the more accurate methods available indicate that the oldest rocks on earth, Zircon grains of rocks from western Australia, are about 4,200 million years old. Meteorites have been found with ages about 4,600 million years and it is concluded that the earth and the meteorites were formed about the same time.

COMPARISON WITH "BIBLICAL" AGES

Such a discrepancy with the 6,000 years from the literal interpretation of the Bible has led some biblical literalists, rather unconvincingly, to a revision of the meaning of "days" in the Bible. Genesis chapter 1 is very precise with its repeated refrain, "And there was evening and there was morning, the [first-sixth] day." Note that six "days" are provided for the creation of the whole universe, including the earth, before Adam was formed. On this basis each "day" would be, from modern evidence, about 2,000 million years.

It is then pointed out that the creation of humans, rather than the creation of the universe, could have been only 6000 "years" ago. Fossil remains, dated by rock strata, indicate that humans, *Homo sapiens*, first appeared about 200,000 years ago. To make this agree with the sum of the ages of recorded generations requires the "years" in the human ages to be about thirty-five years each, making the scriptural ages of Methuselah and his relations into 35,000 years each, which is difficult to believe.

The evidence from radioactivity is particularly important in refuting the beliefs of "creationists," who still take the Bible account of creation literally. They claim that the Flood in the time of Noah invalidates arguments for the age of the earth from the sedimentation of rocks. Radioactivity is not affected by floods or other changes of chemical environment, or by changes of the earth's temperatures.

I have dealt with this matter in some detail since there are many Christians, especially in the United States, who still cling to the literal account of creation in Genesis and disbelieve the results of geologists. As recently as spring 2001 a bill was introduced in Louisiana preventing the state government from distributing "false" information—such as radiometric dating.

The full picture of the dating of rocks and sediments is vital for the dating of fossils found in those rocks and sediments, which provides evidence of the evolution of animals and plants.

CHAPTER 8

Biological Evolution

THE MENTION of the word *evolution* has a disturbing effect on many Christians. When asked to explain what it means to them, they will, in nearly every instance, say that it is a scientific theory about the origin of humankind, or perhaps in more emotional terms, "that man is descended from monkeys." On pointing out that there are other aspects of evolution, such as the physical evolution of the universe, the geological evolution of the earth, and the evolution of plants and animals, some boldly but illogically disbelieve all aspects of evolution. Others are prepared to believe that plants and animals evolved but reject the idea that humans also evolved. We are at the apex of the evolutionary sequences, endowed with many features that put us above other animals. The main differences concern our brains and their greatly superior intellectual ability, and our ability to store information in our memories and communicate by speech. Humans also appear to have unique senses of beauty, spiritual values, and the art of creativity. One element in this rejection of the identity of humans that will require closer examination is the claim that humans possess souls, and animals do not. The evidence concerning this is discussed in chapter 12.

Darwin's book *On the Origin of Species by Means of Natural Selection* was sold out on its publication day, November 24, 1859. His views on the evolution of humans were set out in his *The Descent of Man* in 1871. Darwin's grandfather had written an earlier and more speculative account of evolution, and likewise Lamarck had written in similar terms in 1809. More remarkably, Alfred Wallace (1823–1913) was writing at about the same time as Darwin on "natural selection." He communicated with Darwin and they produced a joint publication in July 1858. What was so striking about Darwin's work was his meticulous sifting of a large variety and volume of evidence, and his ordering of species with sequences of intermediary forms. But even more remarkable was the plausible mechanism for evolution of species—natural selection within and between species. Malthus in 1838 had suggested natural selection within a species, but not between species, noting that selection by humans had led to dramatic changes in domestic animals, for example, among dogs. This "human selection" with "micro evolution" is a small-scale equivalent of "natural selection" leading to "macroevolution." Herbert Spencer, about 1855, was the first to coin the phrase "survival of the fittest."

It is important to distinguish between evidence for the evolution of species and evidence for the mechanism by which this is achieved. The identification, by observations in nature, of series of species believed to be uniquely linked, has been confirmed by studies of the genetic code evidenced by the molecule DNA (short for deoxyribonucleic acid), its structure having been discovered in 1953. This is a double helix, like a twisted ladder, having rungs made up of base pairs of only four different "half-rungs." The helical lines holding the rungs together have two molecules for each rung, a sugar molecule to which the rungs are attached alternating with a phosphate molecule. The four half-rungs are chemical bases—adenine, thiamine, guanine, and cytosine—and they join up in pairs as AT (or TA) and CG (or GC). The very long lengths of double helix, some 3,000 million base pairs in a typical DNA molecule, provide enormous numbers of codes for different proteins.

Treating the DNA molecule as a "library" of information, the base pairs are the four letters of the genetic alphabet, forming sentences corresponding to the 30,000 or more human "genes" with each containing an average of about 100,000 letters, or base pairs. These genes govern physical characteristics and genetically influenced behavior, and are arranged on twenty-three pairs of chromosomes, visible using a microscope, forty-six "volumes" in the "library," one of which can be male or female. Three base pairs taken together provide a code for a particular amino acid, and a string of bases taken together translates into a particular protein. Proteins can make thousands of different structures with specific roles such as carrying oxygen from the lungs through the bloodstream, or stiffening fingernails.

This genetic code appears to be universal, the same base triplets code for the same amino acids in all forms of life on earth, both plants and animals. By splitting DNA along its length to form what is known as RNA (ribonucleic acid), it is easy for replication of a DNA molecule to take place in a suitable chemical environment. The RNA also takes part in the generation of specific amino acids, leading to specific proteins.

The whole sequence for humans has been studied, and the Human Genome Project, studying some 30,000 or more genes, was completed earlier than predicted, in 2002, after fifteen years of research. Some 98 percent of the human genome is identical with the genetically nearest animal to humans, namely the chimpanzee.

The evolutionary sequence of plants or animals does not follow a single line. It is more like a "tree of life" as first sketched by Darwin in 1837. Details of the relationships between species are still being studied. Nevertheless already a widespread conviction exists that the evidence for evolution is beyond reasonable doubt. There used to be special emphasis, by those not convinced of the theory, on the gaps in several sequences, particularly the sequence leading to human beings. Some Christians used this as evidence for the biblical story of "special creation" of each and every species. Over the decades, however, many missing species have been identified, often in new fossils, and the danger of believing in a "God of the gaps" is now well known. As each gap "reserved" for God is closed, such a God seems to be progressively squeezed out.

These difficulties have not altogether gone away. "Natural selection by survival of the fittest" is the principal mechanism used to support evolution in nature. Other mechanisms, such as "sexual selection" (see chapter 17), have been suggested, including the inheritance of acquired characteristics. This particular theory, held by Lamarck around 1810–1820, and at first supported by Darwin, led to the excesses of the discredited Russian scientist Lysenko in the 1950s, and is now only of limited interest. The overall conclusion is that genetic information flows outwards from DNA and not inwards for a particular animal; that is, the normal environment does not affect the DNA, but nuclear radiation and some chemicals can produce significant changes in DNA, if only of one base pair, leading to changes in the offspring.

Another area for continuing discussion and study relates to the evolution of such intricate and specific organs as the eye. Similarly a particularly interesting matter is the observation of altruism in animals. In humans we recognize it, and perhaps we do not like to agree that it is evidence for closer links to animals than that portrayed by simple-minded evolutionary mechanisms.

Good geological and fossil evidence exists of five periods of catastrophic mass extinction, the earliest being about 650 million years ago in Mexico. Another, 250 million years ago, killed 95 percent of the shallow water marine organisms, and 75 percent of land-based plants and animal life. No extraterrestrial object appears to have caused these two events. The latest mass extinction was 65 million years ago, almost certainly caused by the collision of a meteorite, a fragment of an asteroid, up to 10 kilometers across, in the Yucatan Peninsula, Mexico, which led to the extinction of dinosaurs and 70 percent of the then-known species. Enormous dinosaurs, and smaller species that evolved into birds, won in the competition with mammals, but the few of the latter that survived this event continued to evolve, eventually arriving at *Homo sapiens*. Dinosaurs did not re-evolve, but crocodiles survived.

DATES FOR THE FIRST HUMANS

There is increasingly clear agreement among scientists concerning the date of the arrival of *Homo sapiens* in the evolutionary sequence. Evidence is given by fossils of human bones, and two principal difficulties have to be faced. The first and most obvious is deciding when to label a fossil as *Homo sapiens*. The second is the dating of the remains.

The evolution of species, as already mentioned, does not usually proceed along a single line. There are forks in the lines, and one of these forks may progress further and the other may die out. Neanderthals, with low sloping foreheads, large brow ridges, and large faces without

chins, are now considered to be too primitive to be the linear ancestors of modern humans. From DNA studies, it appears they have followed a line that diverged some 500,000 years ago from the
evolutionary line leading to *Homo sapiens*. They were in evidence in
Europe from about 120,000 to 30,000 years ago at which time Neanderthals disappear from the fossil record.

In 2003 conclusions were published from the 1997 unearthing of
three skulls in Herto, Ethiopia. They were named *Homo sapiens idaltu*
(*idaltu* means "elder" in the local Afar language), and were identified as
a subspecies of *Homo sapiens*, clearly related to modern man, which is
another subspecies named *Homo sapiens sapiens*. DNA analysis suggests
that *Homo sapiens* evolved in Africa between 200,000 and 150,000
years ago. Argon-argon radioactive dating of the volcanic ash in which
the three skulls were found established that all three people died
between 160,000 and 154,000 years ago. The previous oldest remains
are dated about 130,000 years ago, from Omo Kibish, in Ethiopia.
Homo sapiens is known to have arrived in the Middle East about 115,000
years ago and reached Europe between 35,000 and 30,000 years ago.
There is no evidence of separate evolution of *Homo sapiens* outside
Africa.

In October 2004 archaeologists reported the discovery of the skele-
ton of a woman aged about thirty years who died about 18,000 years
ago in a large limestone cave on the remote Indonesian island of Flo-
res. Her skull was much smaller than normal, smaller than that of most
chimpanzees, and her height was only about three feet. Seven other
"dwarf humans" were found with evidence that these people lived in a
cave from at least 95,000 to 13,000 years ago. They crafted stone tools,
roasted pygmy elephants, and built rafts, implying that they had a language. They were members of a new human species, named *Homo flore-
siensis*, on a branch of the path of human evolution that diverged from
the path leading to *Homo sapiens* more than a million years ago. This new
branch included *Homo erectus*, formed about 840,000 years ago, found
in Africa, Asia and Europe, and led to this new species.

CHAPTER 9

The Genesis Story of Creation

THE CREATION of the universe is a subject that leads to confrontation with those who still believe that the Book of Genesis contains a God-given literal account of creation. A distinction needs to be drawn between what the Genesis story tells us about the creation of the physical universe, and what it tells us about God and his relation to humankind. The writers or compilers lived between 400 and 1000 years B.C.E., and were doubtless influenced by much older oral traditions. It is difficult for most people to believe that the text is the literal word of God, requiring the text to be believed exactly as it stands.

There are well-known contradictions in the Genesis text. For example "two great lights" we now call the sun and moon are said to be created on the fourth day (v. 16) "to rule over" day and night but there was light and darkness on the first day. This suggests that "day" does not mean twenty-four hours. Rather than dwell on such inconsistencies, it is perhaps wiser to look on the Genesis account of physical creation as the best that could be known at that time, the best indeed that God could possibly reveal to humans at that time as their ability to discover and understand was still evolving. Indeed, other contemporaneous accounts are less convincing. The remarkable aspects of the Genesis story of physical creation are first that God did not snap his metaphorical fingers to create everything in a moment. He took time, nominally six days. The second point is that in the period of creation he chose to create some objects and phenomena before others and then some living creatures before others. It does not require much imagination to find in some of these sequences very approximate parallels to the sequences found in the scientific evidence for physical and biological evolution.

The underlying belief that humankind was the prime purpose of creation is made clear in Gen. 1:27, "God created humankind in his own image; in the image of God he created them; male and female he created them." Some read this to mean that male and female are to be found together in the nature or person of God. Others deduce that men and women are of equal importance, but others still hold to the long-standing belief, reflected in the older account of Genesis 2, that women are secondary to men. Indeed some people still really believe the story of the creation of Eve from one of the ribs of Adam, "by divine surgery under a divine anesthetic," as one notable writer puts it. However, very strong evidence, part of that leading to the theory of biological evolution, indicates that many creatures procreated their next generation by bisexual reproduction a long time before, and right up to, the first human-like people. Most people accept this evidence as being sufficiently reliable to use it as the basis for their Christian belief that men and women coexisted from the very beginning of humankind. The stories of first the forming of Adam and then the miraculous generation of Eve cannot in consequence be literally true, and therefore should not be believed.

The phrase "in the image of God he created them" is usually understood to relate to such characteristics as self-awareness, awareness of others, moral awareness (= conscience), sense of the spiritual, capacity to love, to form relationships and to forgive, intelligence, memory, ability to communicate, conceptual reasoning, and also, in a limited sense, creativity. Some would add capacity to suffer. The question then arises, "How did the writer know that God was like that?" If it is said that God revealed what he was like to humans, in what terms did he communicate? Would it not be rather in the way all good teaching progresses, from the already known to the next stage? The known was, of course, humanity's knowledge of itself. That suggests that the message or revelation would be in the form "I, God, am like you (at your best!)." Could it be that humans over many generations became increasingly aware that they themselves possessed these characteristics, usually in a rudimentary or imperfect fashion? Believing initially in powerful local or specific gods, they projected these elements, expressed as perfect and complete characteristics, into their picture of what the unique creator God must be like. That could well be the way a loving God would choose to reveal himself, a method typical of a good teacher, as God most surely can be assumed to be.

Later, based on the confidence of awe-inspired reasoning, prime characteristics were conceived of as in some sense "infinite." The titles "Omnipotent" and "Omniscient" were introduced and also the qualities Perfectly Good and Immortal. These titles came to generate a range of theological problems, including such topics as natural disasters and diseases, and belief in free will. It was believed that God must have created humankind as perfectly good and immortal. The need to explain how humans became sinful led to the story of the Fall and the consequent loss of immortality. Many believe that God is "Omnipresent" in his creation, for that does not lead to acute theological problems, but rather provides much inspiration and comfort to humankind.

CHAPTER 10

Today's Creation Story: January 1, 2000

THE GENESIS ACCOUNT of creation can be rewritten to allow for increased knowledge of the processes of evolution, while preserving the divine truths of the Bible. The Big Bang and subsequent physical and biological evolution are firmly established beliefs in the minds of nearly all scientists. When set side by side with the account of Creation in Genesis they appear to give a more convincing account of the material creation. But the two accounts have different purposes—the scientific account of course makes no mention of God, but Genesis is primarily concerned with the divine truths of God and his Creation and his relation to humankind. Those parts of Genesis that reveal primitive ideas about the material aspects of Creation can be revised without disturbing most of those divine truths. There is much evidence in the Bible of the evolution of the concept of God, particularly in the Old Testament, but belief in him as Creator and our dependence on him can remain firm and unchanged. In the light of present scientific knowledge, and of subsequent events in history, perhaps the writers of Genesis, inspired by God's continuing revelation of himself, would have written something like this:

> In the beginning, God said "Let there be. . .," and he created the unified forces of physics, with perfect symmetry, and prescient precision.
>
> And out of nothing, and into nothing, God, by a free decision, set up the spontaneous production of particles, in newborn space and time, producing a silent, seething sphere, infinitesimally small, and unimaginably hot.
>
> *There was evolution and emergence*[1] *(p. 84) the first stage of Creation.*
> During a tiny fraction of a second, an expansion took

place, and the perfect symmetry of the forces was broken, step by step, as the temperature dropped, to produce the forces of nature we know today.

God's well-tuned laws made innumerable particles, of every requisite kind, in a steadily expanding chaotic cooling sphere. And the universe cooled for nearly a million years, until electrons could stay joined to nuclei to form familiar atoms.

There was evolution and emergence, the second stage of Creation.

With atoms and molecules as building blocks, the attracting force of gravity took over, and after about a thousand million years, God saw the first stars and galaxies forming in an expanding cosmic universe.

There was evolution and emergence, the third stage of Creation.

Individual stars contracted under gravity, and became hot enough for nuclear fusion to produce chemical elements not seen before, until, after about eight thousand million years, stars were exhausted by their radiance, and God saw them begin to die, some dramatically, by exploding as supernovae, releasing all the chemical elements known today.

There was evolution and emergence, the fourth stage of Creation.

And God saw that it was very good, for now all the ingredients were available, and gravity formed a second generation of stars, some accompanied by planets and satellites, including the sun, earth and, later, the moon, in our galaxy of the Milky Way.

There was evolution and emergence, the fifth stage of Creation.

Bathed in alternate daylight and darkness, during the next thousand million years or so, conditions on earth became favorable for the eventual generation of life.

There was evolution and emergence, the sixth stage of Creation.

During these last three thousand million years, life has evolved as God intended, and through numerous cycles of birth, survival, procreation and death, species have multiplied and progressed, plants and animals of every kind, and some have become extinct. Then, a mere three hundred thousand years ago, there arrived, in the likeness of God, *Homo sapiens*, intelligent humans, with freedom to choose, living together in community, knowing good and evil, pleasure and pain, aware of honor due to their dominion, and acquainted with death.

There was evolution and emergence, the seventh stage of Creation, and the universe entered the Age of Humanity.

Human beings have hardly changed in physical form, during the last 40,000 years, but their knowledge has grown, their understanding has deepened and their beliefs have developed.

And God saw that it was good, but it was not good enough, for free will led to sin and suffering, and guilt and disbelief could lead to despair and the death of the human spirit.

So God sent his only Son, the Word made flesh, who dwelt among us, as Jesus of Nazareth, suffered, died and was raised from the dead, and showed his glory, full of grace and truth.

And that was the beginning of the New Creation.

NOTE

1. *Emergence* is the term used to describe the formation of new, often more complex, structures in physical systems and living organisms. An extreme example is the arrival of consciousness, or self-awareness, which as far as we know appears to have no elementary or rudimentary equivalent in preceding organisms. It is just one of the features appearing or "emergent" in higher levels of the organization of matter.

CHAPTER 11

More Genesis Stories

THE PENTATEUCH AND THE DATING OF GENESIS 1–11

THE PENTATEUCH, the first five books of the Bible, is generally agreed to contain material from at least four sources: (1) The lively passages that refer to God as *Yahweh*, from Judah sources (J), probably written in the ninth century B.C.E.; (2) those with a more measured style, referring to God as *Elohim,* probably deriving from the Northern tribes (E), dated a little later; (3) the exuberant and rhetorical Deuteronomic material (D), found in the Temple in the time of Josiah (640–609 B.C.E.); and (4) the Priestly, legislative and ritual passages (P), compiled during the Exile (597 + 586–539 B.C.E.) using ancient material. J and E were probably combined after the fall of the northern kingdom in 722 B.C.E.; D was added after Josiah, and P was then added after the return from the Exile in 538 B.C.E.

In the first story of Creation, from the Priestly writer(s), in Gen. 1–2:4a, the Hebrew for God is the plural *Elohim*. In the distinctive second story or folktale of Creation, Gen. 2:4b-3:24, generally attributed to J, the original Hebrew for God had no vowels, and came to be known as the tetragrammaton yhwh or jhvh. In the Hellenistic period after about the third century B.C.E., the name was considered too holy for ordinary humans to speak, although it was read aloud by the priests, with a pronunciation now lost, but probably with the vowels from Adhonai (Adonai or adonay) meaning Lord. The Massoretes in the fifth to sixth centuries C.E. supplied the text with the vowels of Adhonai and, about 1520 C.E., Christians coined the name Jehovah for reasons that were not universally accepted at the time. In Exodus 2 the English is usually given as "the LORD God" (the capitals for lord meaning that the Hebrew is yhwh), with the Jerusalem Bible using "Yahweh God."

The discovery of the "book of the law," believed to be Deuteronomy, or at least its chapters 6–28, is reported in 2 Kings 22:8. "The high priest Hilkiah said to Shaphan the secretary, 'I have found the book of the law in the house of the Lord [i.e., the Temple]' and Shaphan (v. 10) "read it aloud to the king." The king was Josiah, king of Judah, 640–609 B.C.E. This book is also referred to as "the book of the covenant" (2 Kings 23:2), as read by Moses to the people (Exod. 24:7). The ambiguous phrases "book of the law of Moses" (Josh. 8:31, 2 Kings 14:6), and "book of the covenant," are sometimes taken to mean all of the first five books of the Bible, also sometimes termed the Torah (= Law). The meaning of Torah is wider than simply Law; it covers much other material, including stories, better termed "Instruction." The forthright character of Josiah probably led to the acceleration of the assembling and revision of the whole of the Torah, including material relating to the Temple and its sacrifices, which began in the ninth century and continued until the fifth or sixth century B.C.E.

The Exile in Babylon provided opportunities to continue this compilation and revision of the Pentateuch. In particular it made the Jews comparatively aware of the beliefs and mythological traditions of Babylonians. The Persian king, Cyrus II, who occupied Babylon in 539 B.C.E., allowed the Jews to return to Jerusalem and reconstruct the Temple and, from 525–515 B.C.E., mostly in the reign of Darius (522–486), the Temple was rebuilt.

The Pentateuch, with its accounts stretching from the Creation itself to the death of Moses, was believed from the beginning of the Christian era to have been largely written by Moses, using contemporary sources. As late as 1902, the Pontifical Biblical Commission maintained the "substantial" Mosaic authorship of the Pentateuch, but in 1948 it conceded the existence of sources and admitted a gradual growth of the Mosaic laws. These decisions have been influenced by increasing archaeological evidence of the beliefs and religious customs of neighboring civilizations.

Genesis has features in common with Greek histories of the sixth century B.C.E., such as genealogies, and tracing of events back to heroes and actions of the gods. No clear distinction was drawn between "historical facts," myths, and legends in pursuit of their intention to establish an identity for the Greeks as an important people. Israelite historians aimed to restore a flagging sense of national significance following a number of defeats, with a divided kingdom, the loss of the Temple, deportation to Babylon, and at times confusion with strange gods. The basis of their writing is the role of Yahweh as the God of the nation.

Evidence of writing dated later than Moses is found in anachronisms and in literary analysis. Mishnaic Hebrew, in which most of the Pentateuch was written, did not develop until the eighth century B.C.E., some time later than 1000 B.C.E. when Hebrew came to be written with the equivalent of the Phoenician alphabetic script. Phrases such as "the house of David," using the later term *beth* to mean both a house (e.g., Beth-el, House of God) and a family, would have been meaningless until the eighth century B.C.E. Previous to that time, two separate words were used, *bayit* for house and *mispeth* for family.

Money in the form of silver coins is mentioned in connection with Joseph's returning money paid for grain to the sacks of his brothers (Gen. 42:25), and Ahab offering money to Naboth for his vineyard (1 Kings 21:2). The earliest reliable evidence for such money is for coins of Lydia, 650 B.C.E. The oldest coins found in Palestine are dated sixth century B.C.E.

The eighteenth-century B.C.E. Joseph is said to have met Ishmaelites with camels (Gen. 37:25) but there is no evidence for camels in Arabia before 850 B.C.E. The books of the Pentateuch could not have developed into their final form until about the late sixth or early fifth century B.C.E.

INFLUENCE OF BABYLONIAN AND OTHER STORIES IN GENESIS 1–11

The Creation Story

Several similar and contrasting stories of creation are associated with different religions. The Babylonian story relates the creation of the first man in Dilmun, a mythical garden of delight beside the Euphrates in Babylon, the city having been founded about 2000 B.C.E. This parallels the Garden of Eden from which a river flows out, dividing into four branches, one of which is Euphrates (Gen. 2:14). The first woman, like Eve in Genesis (2:21–22), is made from a rib of the first man, and in both stories the man and woman are expelled from the garden because of disobedience to God (Marduk in Babylon).

The second part of the Creation Story in Gen. 2:4b–3:24, with its remarkably human references to God, depends on a much older tradition and reads like an addition to the formal style of Chapter 1. It seems to be separate and is in fact at times contradictory—in Gen. 1:27–28 male and female are created together on the sixth day, but in Gen. 2:7 man (alone) is created: "In the [single?] day that the lord God made the earth and the heavens." Although both stories could have derived from a common source, it is more likely that the Babylonian story was added to an existing Hebrew account.

The Flood

Flood stories are found in many cultures, suggesting that massive local flooding occurred 3,000–4,000 years ago. The story of the Flood in Gen. 6:11–9:17 has close Babylonian and Greek parallels. The Babylonian epic of Gilgamesh, dated about 1600 B.C.E., with Utnapishtim in place of the righteous man Noah, has an ark that comes to rest on a high mountain after the sending out of a raven. The rainbow is also given as an assurance that there will be no more floods. The Greek story has the god Zeus, with Deucalion and his wife Pyrrha, good people warned by his father Prometheus. Their boat landed on Mount Parnassus.

Literary analysis indicates that the Genesis story is a combination of two stories. At one point, the Hebrew for God changes from Yahweh to Elohim (Gen. 6:11–12). There is a discrepancy in the duration of the Flood (Gen. 7:4–8:14) and the two versions are difficult to disentangle. It is suggested that the flood stories arose from an event in the Tigris-Euphrates valley in about 3000 B.C.E., possibly associated with the erupting volcano in the Aleutian Islands with its worldwide consequences (3119 B.C.E.; NC). It is most unlikely that the stories of Noah and Utnapishtim were discovered and combined before the

Exile in Babylon. Uncorroborated claims to have discovered remains of Noah's ark on Mount Ararat may deserve further studies.

The Tower of Babel

Babel is Hebrew for Babylon and means "Gate of God." The Assyrian king Esarhaddon (681–665 B.C.E.) found a centuries-old derelict tower in Babel and began rebuilding it, with the aim of making "the top reach to heaven." The same phrase occurs in Gen. 11:4. The king angered the god Marduk and after five storeys, each eighteen meters high, the building was stopped because of a series of accidents attributed to Marduk. It was believed that he brought contention into the speech of humankind, which until then had been a single language. It seems therefore that the Genesis story was inspired by a real event in Babylon and was probably written later than the seventh century B.C.E.

THE GENESIS STORY OF RIGHT AND WRONG

Genesis 2 is the very human story of the origin of evil and its consequence in death. Again I shall not dwell on those who claim that the eating of an apple was literally the first sin, preferring to agree that the deliberate denial of God's commands is seriously sinful. More significant is to ask how humankind became aware of what they believed to be God's commands. This is similar to the question, "How did humankind know that they were made in the image of God?" For those who think in terms of primitive humans, it is evident that humans certainly developed in pairs and in smaller or larger communities. A sense of right and wrong would have developed as soon as self-identity became a part of experience, together with the recognition that other people existed with their own senses of identity. From time to time the desires of two people would be different, and at times in conflict. Each would be likely to believe that he or she was right and the other wrong. The community, if only for its own protection, would then begin to establish rules concerning right and wrong.

One of the extremes in the spectrum of right and wrong would be the taking of the life of another human, and a pattern of punishments would be developed to fit the crimes. The Jewish principle of "an eye for an eye, and a tooth for a tooth" may well have been one of the first formulated punishment codes.

It is not facetious to point out that in lower animals, such as chimpanzees and even in cats, the parental urge to teach their offspring what is, and is not, acceptable behavior is very evident. It is therefore not unreasonable to believe that the sense of right and wrong for humans evolved and did not have a uniquely timed beginning.

ORIGINAL SIN

The belief that the universe was declared by God to be "very good" (Gen. 1:31) led naturally to the belief that humans were created morally perfect. Their experience of moral imperfection seemed to demand an event of transition from perfection to imperfection, hence the story of the Fall. The "original righteousness" was replaced by "Original Sin." The term in theological parlance refers not to one sinful action but a condition of human nature. The Thirty-nine Articles (Article IX) in the *Book of Common Prayer* states, "It is the fault and corruption of every man, that naturally is engendered of the offspring of Adam; whereby man is very far gone from original righteousness and is of his own nature inclined to evil . . . it deserves God's wrath and damnation"— which is rather hard on a newborn child.

It is surprising that more attention was not paid to changes in attitudes to "inherited sin" between the times of Exod. 20:5 and Ezek. 18:1–4,17 and Jesus in John 9:1–3. We read in Exod. 20:5, "for I the LORD your God am a jealous God, punishing children for the iniquity of parents, to the third and fourth generation of those who reject me." This is flatly rejected in Ezek 18:1–4:

> The word of the LORD came to me: What do you mean by
> repeating the proverb concerning the land of Israel, "The
> parents have eaten sour grapes, and the children's teeth are
> set on edge"? As I live says the Lord God, this proverb shall
> no more be used by you in Israel. Know that all lives are mine;

the life of the parent as well as the life of the child is mine: it
is only the person who sins that shall die.

Jesus is clear in his answer to his disciples when they encountered a
man blind from birth (John 9:1–3) and they asked him, "Rabbi, who
sinned, this man or his parents, that he was born blind?" Jesus answered,
"Neither this man nor his parents," and continued with the remarkable statement, "he was born blind so that God's works might be revealed in him," and he proceeded to make him able to see.

Augustine used the expression *depravatio naturae* (corruption of
nature) in his conflict with Pelagius, who held that Adam's sin injured
no one but himself. Calvin went further and spoke of "total deprava-
tion." It is clear that evidence for these contradictory beliefs was found
in personal reasoning based on individual experiences and local practices, with little regard to the quoted passages from scripture.

The expression "Original Sin" does not occur in the Bible. It was
introduced by Tertullian (c. 160–225 C.E.) as *vitium originis.*" The belief
is said to be implied in the saying of Jesus, "If you then, who are evil,
know how to give good gifts to your children, how much more will the
heavenly Father give the Holy Spirit to those who ask him!" (Luke
11:13). Paul writes in Rom. 5:18, "one man's trespass led to condemnation for all. . . . [b]y the one man's disobedience the many were made
sinners," and in 7:16–17, "it is no longer I that do it, but sin that dwells
within me." More explicitly, the belief is expressed in the first-century
C.E. book of 2 Esdras 3:21–22, "for the first Adam, burdened with an
evil heart, transgressed and was overcome, as were also all who were
descended from him. Thus the disease became permanent." And in
7:118, "For though it was you [Adam] who sinned, the fall was not yours
alone, but ours also who are your descendants." The condition of Original Sin is rarely expressed in terms of possession by a personal devil.
Expressions used in 2 Esdras include *evil heart, evil root, grain of evil seed, evil
thought,* and *(evil) mind.*

The belief is of particular interest because it not only calls for study
of the theological element in its use of "sin" and its "origin," but invites
a study of the belief that this characteristic is inherited in normal

biological human reproduction. The question arises, "Can the study of DNA (the molecule that governs heredity) lead to the identification of a code related to past sins, or, more realistically, is there a code or codes that identify a tendency to sin or crime?" There have been reports of attempts to find evidence of this in DNA, but a convincing conclusion has not been reached.

The belief in, and understanding of, Original Sin is a key element in relation to infant baptism. Again there is no specific reference to this practice in the Bible. Some conclude from references to the baptism of whole families that this included infants, for example, in Acts 16:15, "[Lydia] and her household were baptized," and in 16:33 the local jailer, after an earthquake, washed the wounds of the apostles, and "then he and his entire family were baptized without delay." In 1 Cor. 1:16, Paul writes, "I did baptize also the household of Stephanas," adding that he did not baptize many, and was careful not to baptize in the name of Paul. The discussion in 1 Cor. 7:12–16, relating to the marriage of a Christian to an unbeliever, may imply that no need was felt to baptize children (v. 14). Perceived parallels to the Jewish custom of circumcision may have supported the practice, as in Col. 2:11–12: "In him also you were circumcised with a spiritual circumcision, . . . when you were buried with him in baptism, you were also raised with him." In the *Apostolic Tradition* (c. 215) of St. Hippolytus, the elaborate baptismal liturgy explicitly provides for infant baptism. From Origen to Augustine most of the Church supported the practice but there were disagreements, and Tertullian taught that baptism should be deferred until the candidates "know Christ." After the Reformation, several followings were so strongly of the opinion that infant baptism was wrong that they formed separate churches, such as the United Kingdom Baptist Church in 1612.

THE GENESIS STORY OF THE ORIGIN OF DEATH

The very phrase "origin of death" sounds unreasonable to anyone believing in evolution, for the whole process of biological evolution depends on numerous successive cycles of birth, survival, procreation, and death. For those who believe in a creator God, who chose evolution to be the process throughout the universe, there is no escape from the argument that God knew that death, physical death, would be an essential part of the process. It is possible that the horrendous crime of murder, which the Jews punished by the death of the murderer, led to the belief that death for all humans, good and not so good, was the divine punishment of an angry God for some primeval sin. A creator God who was the God of a nation, and defended its territory, was readily accorded such powerful attributes. To many Christian believers, deeply influenced by the loving God of Jesus, with significant elements of justice and mercy, it is a travesty of their "image of God" to believe that he would punish the whole human race with death because one of the hitherto innocent early members of that race disobeyed perceived commands. Death was part of God's plan for the evolution of humankind. And so was animal suffering and death.

IMMORTALITY OF THE SOUL

The meaning of the word "death" in scripture is worth a special study. For the Hebrews, death meant "being gathered to one's fathers," and part of the fear that attended it was separation from their God. Death was not seen as "natural" but as evil, as in Deut. 30:15, 19: "See, I have set before you today life and prosperity, death and adversity." The fear of death among the Hebrews, as for other primitive peoples, was not connected with the thought of utter annihilation but stems from a belief that there is some kind of life after death, which, for some people, can be filled with torment and eternal punishment. This is borne out by the story of a rich man who was wickedly unkind to a poor man, Lazarus (Luke 16:19–31). Lazarus "was carried away by the angels to be with Abraham." "The rich man saw Abraham far away with Lazarus by his side" and begged Abraham to have mercy "for I am in agony in these flames."

Physical death as a consequence of sin is frequently referred to in the Bible, especially in the New Testament, for example, Rom. 6:23, "the wages of sin is death," and 1 Cor. 15:56, "the sting of death is sin." The belief that humans were originally created not only perfect, free from sin, but also "immortal," free from death, may well have been the result of speculation on what would have happened if the first humans had not sinned. Immortality, inability to die, was perhaps seen as an aspect of their being made in the image of God. On the other hand, the writer of Gen. 3:22 makes clear his belief that God saw that the "fallen man" had obtained, by eating the apple, a knowledge of good and evil and "might reach out his hand and take also from the tree of life [in the Garden of Eden, Gen. 2:9], and eat, and live for ever." There is no mention that he did so, and to prevent him from doing so is given (3:23) as one of the reasons for the expulsion of Adam and Eve from the garden.

About the time of the transportation of Israelites to Babylon, (the Exiles, 597 and 586–538 B.C.E.), there was a developing belief that the human soul was immortal. This shift in the significance of death is an example of the development of belief, and the evidence that supported it is a good topic for study. Most commentators feel that the experience of the Exile, with a belief that God would not abandon his people, is part of their growing awareness, coupled possibly with encountering a revised notion of immortality, that is, life after death, among the Babylonians and other peoples.

Spiritual Death

In contrast to the everyday use of death in a clear physical sense, death in the Bible is also accorded a symbolic significance. This is particularly evident in the New Testament where Christians are told in Eph. 2:1, "You were dead through the trespasses and sins in which you once lived." This cannot be physical death, and it is sometimes referred to as "spiritual death," although that term does not occur in the Bible. Instead there are references to spiritual life—"the letter [i.e., the Law] kills, but the Spirit gives life" (2 Cor. 3:6). The term *spiritual death* has a ring of finality, although in 1 John 5:16–17 we read, "There is sin that is mortal … but there is sin that is not mortal." Perhaps it would be better to introduce the idea of "spiritual sickness" from which it would be possible to recover, by confession and forgiveness, contrition, and, where possible, restitution. There would seem to be an attempt to define spiritual death in 1 John 3:14, "whoever does not love abides in death."

The development of beliefs from the Old Testament to the New leads to an attempt to reconcile difficult OT beliefs by treating them as allegories, seeing them as forerunners of some of the more acceptable expressions in the New Testament. This needs to be done with special care as references to the death of Jesus is most obviously meant to refer to his physical death. So in 1 Cor. 15:21–22 we read, "For since death came through a human being, the resurrection of the dead has also come through a human being, for as all die in Adam so all will be made alive in Christ." We may wish to take this to mean "for since spiritual death came through a human being," but we cannot go on to say "the resurrection of the spiritually dead" in reference to Jesus. Or can we? It has been suggested that on the cross Jesus died both physically and spiritually, having taken to himself the burden of the sins of others, though he had no sin himself. It is still worth being explicit by countering the long-standing but erroneous belief that physical death came into the world because of sin, as unambiguously expressed in Rom. 5:15, "the many died through the one man's trespass." It is a measure of the changing of human ideas concerning the creator that today few people would suggest that God was so offended by the eating of an apple by one human that he condemned to physical death the whole of humankind.

EVIDENCE PROVIDED BY EARLY GENESIS STORIES

The Hebrews loved stories, and Jesus used stories to answer some of the difficult questions put to him. "Who is my neighbor?" is answered by the story of the good Samaritan (Luke 10:29–37). He illustrated God the Father's love in the story of the Prodigal Son (Luke 15:11–32). Genesis stories need to be interpreted in a similar way, by identifying their purpose and carefully avoiding a literal interpretation.

The evidence provided by the early stories in Genesis is primarily evidence of the beliefs of their authors or editors. Some of these stories are attempts to explain the beliefs of contemporaries concerning

the nature of humans and the nature of God. The creation stories provide an answer to the question "How did we come to exist?" and assume
there is one God, all powerful, with the highest level of morality, and
prepared to punish sinners severely. He is also believed to be able to
communicate with humans and to have concern for their well-being.
For example, when Adam and Eve realized they were naked, "the Lord
God made garments of skins for the man and for his wife, and clothed
them" (3:21). Many other details in the story indicate how similar to
humans God was believed to be. Thus in 3:8, "They heard the sound of
the Lord God walking in the garden at the time of the evening breeze."
There is another point to this story of the Fall—it tells of how blame
is put on somebody else, Adam blames Eve, and Eve blames Satan.
Many people do the same today, and ultimately blame the Devil for
their wrongdoing, when they ought to accept that the temptation and
the deed itself both can be from within.

The story of the formation of Eve from a rib of Adam (2:21–23) is
used to explain why "a man leaves his father and his mother and clings
to his wife." Perhaps this is evidence of a matriarchal society, or simply
a recognition of the fact that families split in order to multiply. The
"[increased] pangs of childbearing" are explained as part of God's punishment of Eve for her disobedience (3:16), and the man is told, "cursed
is the ground because of you . . . thorns and thistles it shall bring forth
for you" (3:17–18). Sadly such ideas are still sometimes taught today,
as examples of God's punishment of sin.

The point of the Cain and Abel story is not obvious. It may serve to
indicate that keepers of sheep are of higher status than tillers of the
ground. How the two brothers knew that "the Lord had regard for Abel
and his offering, but for Cain and his offering he had no regard"
(4:4–5) is not revealed, but the fact that Cain could hear the Lord's
question "Why are you angry?" (Gen. 4:6) and later, "Where is your
brother Abel?" (4:9), suggests a belief in direct audio communication,
or conversations in the mind. The punishment for Cain is poorer
yields from tilling the ground and condemnation to life as a fugitive.
However, there is a touch of mercy when God says, "Whoever kills
Cain will suffer a sevenfold vengeance" (Gen. 4:15). The meaning of

this curse is not clear. The point of the story may be that it is evidence of the increase of evil and the emphasis is on the seriousness of murder. If so, this must be before the establishment of "an eye for an eye."

The story of Noah and the Flood makes the point that God is angered by sin and inflicts punishment. There is also an indication of the mercy of God, at least for Noah and his family. When it says in Gen. 6:5, "the Lord saw that the wickedness of humankind was great in the earth, and that every inclination of the thoughts of their hearts was only evil continually," this must reflect what humans were beginning to think, and they expected dire consequences. A further example of anthropomorphism follows (6:6): "And the Lord was sorry that he had made humankind on the earth, and it grieved him to his heart." The fact that there are parallel flood stories in other countries lends support to the belief that there really was some kind of widespread disaster. An existing tradition appears to have been adapted to illustrate beliefs about the reaction of God to human sin. Such reactions are more like the reactions of humans who have suffered the sins of other humans. We may not be so easily persuaded that this is what God is really like.

The story of the tower of Babel may also stem from an actual happening, but the point of the story is to explain why there are so many different languages among humans. The basis of the story is the conviction that humans before sinning spoke a single language, and some disastrous punishment led to the multiplicity of languages, with no evidence of God's mercy. The cause is said to be the builders' aim to make the "top reach to heaven," which would displease God in heaven. This is evidence of how heaven was pictured in the age of the authors. It has to be admitted that there are some Christians today who still believe that heaven is "up there," the dwelling of God.

The aims of the writers and compilers of Genesis and later books almost certainly included the creation or restoration of a sense of national identity, badly injured by a variety of battles, deportations, and the destruction of the Temple and other places of worship. The strength of these aims lay in a clear-cut monotheism expressed in a culture in which the role of God was explicitly central. That heritage became the foundation for the Incarnation and the spread of the Christian church.

Apart from some general considerations, such as the implication that sin angers God and leads to punishment, sometimes tempered with mercy, there is not much evidence in these stories concerning what Christians should believe today. Some are most unlikely to be based on historical events. It is true that humans often behave today in ways similar to those portrayed in these stories. Beliefs about the nature of God have, however, developed. The role of the love of God and the effects of the Incarnation and Atonement (see chapter 16) make some of the actions of God described in these stories scarcely believable. The stories depend on the deep-seated beliefs of the writers and give evidence of how much more developed is the New Testament understanding of God.

CHAPTER 12

Person—Material, Mental, Spiritual

BODY AND MIND

WHEN WE CONSIDER what it is to be a person, a number of words enter our thoughts—body, mind, soul, spirit. There can be few recognitions of the meaning of these words more clear and poignant than that afforded by the sight and touch of a dead person. Here is a body, able to be studied as a material object, if so desired. However, a body is in no sense a complete person.

If the body is now considered to be endowed with life, a whole new range of reality is encountered. We recognize the potential for action; breathing, eating, speaking, interactions with others, and reproduction of the next generation. What the living body is can now be identified, in part, by what that body does. That a human being is more than other animals is recognized by the power to communicate in great detail, ability to remember in detail, evidence of ability to reason to a wide range of levels, together with many activities such as the use of tools, creation of symbolic objects, and objects distinguishable solely for their beauty. The power to communicate using a developed language has a special quality as it enables us to conclude that there are other humans with similar characteristics, and the practice of living in community becomes the norm. We ask questions about what it is to be human not only in terms of our own individual experience but also in terms of what others have to tell us. We recognize that there are important differences between persons, not least when we have cause to express differences of opinion that may need to be resolved, or at least to be the subject of deep-thinking inquiry. We have not considered the significance of self-awareness, partly because it is difficult to decide whether or not some animals possess it. Domestic animals seem at times to show characteristics that are "almost human." For my present purpose we have no need to pursue this matter.

What we do recognize, in ourselves and in others, is that we think. This activity is not only associated with words and self-determined logical progression, but also involves emotions, intuition, imagination, and invention. Descartes (1596–1650) considered that thinking proved that he existed, *cogito ergo sum*, "I think therefore I am." Others question the logic of concluding about a state of being from what is an activity. It might be more acceptable to say, "I think therefore I am becoming" (*cogito ergo fio*). It is this sense of "becoming" that makes us conclude that we are both alive and have a potentiality to think, and this leads to a sense of freedom of will. We then ask what it is about ourselves that enables us and others to think, and, long before the present-day understanding of the brain, we said that we have a "mind." It follows that differences between people implies different minds and hence a person is characterized by his or her mind as well as the appearance of that person's body. It does not follow that the "mind" is a separately identifiable entity. It is sufficient to note that the evolving brain supports "mental" activity. But see the papal comment on p. 42.

Are then body and mind enough to identify a person? The extreme materialist may claim that they are, and some would go further and state their belief in the possibility of explaining self-awareness, patterns of thinking, awareness of beauty and goodness, creativity, and other human activity solely in terms of body and mind, maybe even avoiding the use of the word *mind* and concentrating on the brain and mental processes. The difference between a suitably designed computer and the brain of a human being exercises the thinking of many scientists today. The possibility of designing such a computer is often doubted.

The relation of mind to body is much debated. Descartes conceived of the mind as an entity in its own right, a "mental substance" compared with the body as a material substance. This substance dualism is now largely discarded, and it is claimed by some that mind cannot exist without matter. Some philosophers believe that the relation of mind to body is an insoluble problem.

SPIRIT AND SOUL

Beyond the recognition of body and its mental processes, many wish to introduce human spirituality, but we need to be cautious because of the different meanings and interpretations that such concepts invite. At one extreme are those who identify spirit as if it were an "entity" distinct from the body. Some go further and believe that, at some point in the evolution of humans, spirit was suddenly and explicitly added to the individual, but not necessarily as a "substance." This inner, vital, and spiritual principle, which relates to the body-mind, is termed the *soul* or *spirit*. The person is then said to consist of body, mind, and soul (sometimes body, mind, and spirit), without overimplied distinction between body and mind. This is essentially the position adopted by those who wish to give importance to certain aspects of the second account of creation in Genesis, "the Lord God . . . breathed into his nostrils the breath of life; and the man became a living being" (Gen. 2:7). They assert therefore that this act of God made a clear distinction between humans and animals, and implies that an animal does not have a "soul." It is also used by some to indicate the point at which humans became uniquely and fully human, with purported original innocence, ignorance of right and wrong, no sense of good and evil, fashioned with perfection and favored with immortality.

Some people nowadays cling to this belief in order to rescue what remains of the Genesis account of the creation of humans, when evolution is taken into account, in order to lead into a belief in the Fall and its consequences. The belief in a separate addition of soul (or spirit), by divine intervention, has a profound affect on the theology of sin and death, and of such difficult ideas as Original Sin; consequently, it influences attempts to understand the work of Jesus in relation to atonement. It is perilously close to a "God of the gaps," making a gap that, to scientists, is unnecessary, in order to let God in. It links to a controversial belief that evolution leaves no room for God in creation and a gap is therefore needed. It could also have arisen from the traditional belief, now often challenged, that God governed and continues to govern the whole process of evolution, step by step, and likewise events in the earth and universe today, so that any attempt to explain the process is unnecessary.

The most important basis of the theory of evolution is the identification of a sequence of events, with branching, parallel developments, and extinctions, and the production of a corresponding time scale. The process of evolution is necessarily a matter of speculation, a hypothesis based on observation and reasoning, for there is no way in which we can experiment adequately to test the hypothesis. It is still accepted by most scientists that survival of the fittest and adaptation to the environment seem to be the most important of cooperating processes. The evidence for the belief held by some Christians that God guided, and still guides, evolution, is not immediately obvious or necessary in biological terms. It is a belief that cannot be proved unreasonable if the scale of the guiding is not defined. The extent to which the proposed guiding would constitute the breaking of natural law is not clear.

The principal alternative to literal interpretation of the parts of the Genesis creation story involving divine intervention is provided by the extension of evolution of the whole universe, physical and biological, to the evolution of what it is to be human, what it is to be a person. As the human body evolved, so did the mind, the mental processes of the brain, and there seems to be no need to exclude the evolution of the sense of spirituality, coupled with a sense of religious experience. There would then be no point in time when a man was transformed from being an animal to being a person.

The recognition of good and evil, stemming largely from living in community, and the acceptance that death is an essential part of the evolution of living creatures, has been linked by some to the thought that good and evil impulses are introduced from without, rather than conceived from within. External agents are then felt to be different from humans and the concept of "spirit" is claimed to find a place, or rather a wide variety of places, in angels and demons (or evil spirits) that can come and go, a belief that extends to the Devil himself. The things of the spirit, both external and internal, are then at the mercy of logic based on human characteristics and relationships. A complete spiritual world comes into conceptual experience, together with the dangers of moral dualism.

This belief in the continuation of evolution up to a complete human replaces the sections in Genesis that introduce the serpent, later identified as the Devil (Wisd. 2:24), the origin of good and evil, the first sin or Fall, the consequences of that Fall, and in particular death. That is not to deny that there is much else in Genesis that provides valuable food for thought about God and what it is to be human. Continuation of evolution in all aspects of human experience was the dominating thought in the writings of Teilhard de Chardin (1881–1955), the French Jesuit paleontologist, and it is a richly rewarding way to see wholeness in God's creation. His linking of Christian dogma to scientific theory was treated with caution by the Roman Catholic Church.

It would be tedious, and create too much of a divergence, to list and discuss the wide-ranging "evidence" for belief in external spirits found in ancient society as well as in present-day religious societies. Personal experience, and close acquaintance with others who claim such experience, will provide for some the most convincing evidence; indeed the strength of conviction based on that experience will often be so great that attempts to discern differences, and to share conflicting evidence, will largely fail. As a category of evidence, belief in the existence and actions of individual spirits is peculiarly impervious, and seekers without such convincing evidence find themselves treated as if they lack some vital human potential.

SPIRITUAL AND RELIGIOUS EXPERIENCE

Spiritual experience can be defined as a conscious feeling of external power, with no obvious explanation in terms of normal comprehension. Belief in the possibility of divine activity can lead to the feeling that some spiritual experience has divine connections, associated with an awareness of love, and this may then be called religious experience. It is a particular aspect of a more general spiritual experience.

Such experiences have been reported throughout human history by all sorts of people, and they have been dismissed by many people as having little or no significance due to abnormal mental states. The fact remains that studies of the frequency of these experiences among several thousand individuals, made by Sir Alister Hardy in the 1970s, and by others through to 1987, show that about one-half of individuals report some kind of spiritual experience, and many believe them to be religious experiences. Attempts have been made to categorize different aspects of these feelings, including a sense of security, a sense of happiness, a sense of being at one with creation, extra-vivid perception of Nature, a sense of new purpose, and a sense of an internal initiative with an external response, coupled sometimes with a belief in answer to prayer. Some report a visual experience, with "visions" of people or bright lights. Others relate to music or conversations, and yet others to a sense of smell or touch. It is not accepted by most people that this is a dream-like experience, because of the nature of the occasion, for example, that it happens in company and is dissociated from tiredness or sleep. It is a conscious decisionmaking process to have a relationship with God through Christ.

Many individual reports have been given by people, with much detail, and the experience has sometimes led to a significant change in the character of their thoughts, and of their actions in relation to others. I shall confine myself to a report from an unexpected quarter, namely Bertrand Russell, atheist, mathematician, and philosopher (1872–1970). In volume I of his autobiography, 1872–1914, he describes an experience when he was twenty-nine, during a stay with A. N. Whitehead (1861–1947), the British mathematician and philosopher. Mrs. Whitehead suddenly suffered severe pain in her heart, and Russell was aware of a "sense of solitude of each human soul which suddenly overwhelmed" him. Within five minutes of reflection he concluded that

> nothing can penetrate [the loneliness of the human soul] except the highest intensity of the sort of love that religious teachers have preached. . . . At the end of those five minutes, I had become a completely different person. For a time, a sort

of mystic illumination possessed me. . . . Having for years cared only about exactness and analysis, I found myself filled with semi-mystical feelings about beauty. . . . The mystic insight . . . has largely faded, and the habit of analysis had reasserted itself. But something of what I saw in that moment has remained always with me.

AFTER DEATH

The belief in spirit in the context of a person becomes particularly important when questions are asked about what happens to the person when the body dies. Most people are prepared to accept that the material body loses its significance as a part of being a person, as witnessed by the fact that it is buried and decays, in spite of attempts to preserve it by embalming, and sometimes providing food for some time after death. In many cultures the body is cremated. Some faiths believe that in some sense the body will be "resurrected" as distinct from "resuscitated." Paul introduces the term *spiritual body*, as, for example, in 1 Cor. 15:42–54, in a context that is steeped in the imagery of his time.

The key question is "Does the person in any sense exist after death?" not just as a memory among relatives and friends, but as a definable being. Two areas and types of evidence are relevant; the first includes reports of awareness of dead persons (ghosts?), and the second is the widespread belief that there is, in some sense, "life" after death.

For those who believe that there is almost palpable evidence of the interaction of spirituality between living persons, it is natural to believe that this same element of a person continues to exist after death. In almost all religions there is belief in this continuing existence, and the term *soul* then becomes firmly associated with that aspect, element, or principle of a person that continues as an entity after death. Some go further and engage in a belief in reincarnation, but the evidence for that is not easy to find. Claims for reincarnation based on "reason" are not very persuasive for most people, nor are quotations from highly respected adherents to the belief. Evidence of strong similarities between individuals of one generation and the next is usually easy to explain in terms of genetics and environment, although claims to revive detailed memories of a previous existence, if validated, may come into a different category, and the evidence should be properly examined.

In early Judaism, no sharp distinction was made between body and soul. This is referred to as "psychosomatic unity." The long-standing belief was that the person after death went to Sheol, a vague parking place, as in Gen. 37:35, where Jacob, at the supposed loss of Joseph, says, "I shall go down to Sheol to my son, mourning." In the two centuries before Jesus, some Jews, such as the Sadducees, were outspoken in defending that belief, but the Pharisees on the other hand believed in imperishable souls that received immediate reward or punishment for their behavior in this life. In the Old Testament, resurrection after death is explicitly referred to only in Dan. 12:2, "Many of those who sleep in the dust of the earth shall awake, some to everlasting life, and some to shame and everlasting contempt." It was not until the Middle Ages that Jews adopted the developed belief that the soul is the principle of life, capable of surviving the decay of the body.

Plato (c. 428–347 B.C.E.), in *The Republic,* divided the soul into three parts, which roughly correspond to reason, emotion, and desire. He claims in *Phaedrus* that the three parts are together immortal, but in *Timaeus* limits immortality to the reasoning part. The views of later Greek and Roman Platonists, now known as Neoplatonism, are found in the writings of Plotinus (205–270 C.E.). They saw the soul as a prisoner in a material body, and this prevailed in Christian thought until Thomas Aquinas (1224–1274). He accepted the view of Aristotle (384–322 B.C.E.) that soul and body are two conceptually distinguishable elements of a single substance. Most Christians believe that the human personality as a whole, composed of soul (or spirit) and resurrected (spiritual) body, may be granted God's presence in the life after death.

HUMAN PERSON IN THE BIBLE

The people of Israel were at first more concerned with their corporate and national identity than with the individual person. Later, and particularly after the encounter with Hellenism, the nature of the individual became a more prominent concern. The Hebrew word for the human being is *nephesh*, with a wide range of meanings, including both flesh and soul as inseparable components. Animals were considered to be solely flesh (*basar*). At death the flesh dies and the human soul is to dwell in Sheol, a shadowy place for the dead. In Greek thought the body (*soma*) is separate from the soul (*psyche*).

The Hebrew *ruach*, and Greek *pneuma*, translated "spirit," are also used for "breath," which is an agent of God, and more particularly associated with life. In the postexilic period, after 538 B.C.E., spirit and soul became synonymous, the seat of intelligence and emotion in humans. This usage continued into the New Testament period. The early Hebrew belief in "spirits," supernatural beings, alive in woods, stones, and so on, is a legacy from primitive religion. God is believed to control such spirits; later on they included angels, archangels, and a whole hierarchy of good spiritual beings. But it is also believed that there are demons, or supernatural forces of wickedness, such as Jesus is reported as exorcising. The power of human imagination and inventiveness in this connection is almost unlimited.

Heart is a much-used word in the Bible, a word with many nuances. It covers such personal qualities as courage, trust, love, understanding, pleasure, and grief, and can be good or evil. It is used to translate the Hebrew *leb*, which the Septuagint usually renders as the Greek *kardia*. Hebrew has no separate word for "will." In the New Testament, as in the Old, heart is the seat of the reason and will, as well as of the emotions. Key meanings of *heart* are found in Mark 11:23, "do not doubt in your heart, but believe," and in Ezek. 36:26, where the Lord declares to the exiles in Babylon, "I will remove from your body the heart of stone and give you a heart of flesh," that is, endow with compassion. Again, in Deut. 6:4, "You shall love the Lord your God with all your heart, and with all your soul, and with all your might." It is perhaps important to note that Jesus modified this "command" to include the phrase "and all your mind" (Matt. 22:37). It is significant that "heart" relates to love, "mind" relates to truth, and "soul" relates to mystery, three characteristic elements in Christian belief. The use of reason in one's relation to

God is an aspect of belief, and part of the search for evidence. This is an example of the influence of Greek patterns of thought, found from time to time in the recorded sayings of Jesus.

Trust and love go together, as in Prov. 31:11, "The heart of her husband trusts in her," and in Prov. 3:5, "Trust in the Lord with all your heart." In Mal. 4:6 the Lord "will turn the hearts of parents to their children and the hearts of children to their parents." The heart is so evidently a central feature of a person that it overlaps the meaning of "soul," and use of the word *heart* fills out the meaning of the word *soul*.

Paul, remarkably, says of God, "he hardens the heart of whomsoever he chooses" (Rom. 9:18).

CHAPTER 13

Evidence for the Resurrection of Jesus

JEWISH BELIEFS AND PRACTICES

IN ORDER to appreciate evidence in the Bible for belief in the resurrection of Jesus, it is helpful to study the beliefs and practices of the Jews at the time, and in the place where the events took place. There were important changes in the Hebrews' beliefs in the afterlife during the last thousand years B.C.E.

Before the Exile there is limited evidence concerning the afterlife but, like all Near East cultures, persons were believed to continue to exist after death, having gone to Sheol (sometimes translated as "Hell," but also as "pit" in AV and RV). This is made explicit in Num. 16:33: "So they with all that belonged to them went down alive into Sheol; the earth closed over them, and they perished from the midst of the assembly." Archaeological evidence shows that food was buried with the dead, enough for a journey, but food was not provided from time to time as happened in nearby countries. Necromancy, the art of calling up the dead to reveal future events, clearly was believed to take place because it was actively condemned (Isa. 8:19–20), although no reasons for condemnation are given. In 1 Sam. 28:3–19 Saul inquires of the witch of Endor, who calls up Samuel to advise Saul. In Lev. 20:27 we read, "A man or a woman who is a medium or a wizard shall be put to death." During and after the Exile the belief developed that it was impossible to consult the dead.

During and toward the end of the Exile, the Jews grew confident that they would be able to return to their homeland. They remembered the deliverance of the Israelites from Egypt. The hope was for something akin to a corporate "resurrection," a national revival, and this is behind the vision of Ezekiel in chapter 37 with dry bones in a valley being first rearticulated and then covered with flesh, and given life, to form a mighty army. This kind of hope was also expressed for individual persons, particularly good persons, as in Isa. 26:19, "Your dead shall live, their corpses shall rise, O dwellers in the dust, awake and sing for joy! For your dew is a radiant dew, and the earth will give birth to those long dead."

After the Exile, following Alexander the Great's conquest of Palestine in 332 B.C.E., Hellenistic ideas about death and the afterlife, including the Platonic idea of immortality of the soul, are found in Hebrew thought. In the NRSV, Wisd. 3:1, 4, we read "the souls of the righteous are in the hand of God, and no torment will ever touch them . . . their hope is full of immortality." Two distinct ideas exist in the Hellenistic and Roman periods, first the resurrection at the end of time with judgment, reward, and punishment, as in Dan. 12:2, "Many of those who sleep in the dust of the earth shall awake, some to everlasting life, and some to shame and everlasting contempt." (Compare Matt. 27:52.) The second idea is immortality, the immortal soul living on after the death of the body, with immediate reward and punishment. The Pharisees, a school or sect originating in the second century B.C.E., believed in such an imperishable soul and in a bodily resurrection at the Last Judgment, with rewards and punishments. The Sadducees, a well-established group among the Jews of the first century B.C.E., rejected individual resurrection, the afterlife and judgment, and maintained the long-standing belief of the dead being assigned to universal Sheol. They played no significant role in Judaism after the destruction of the Temple in 70 C.E.

BIBLICAL EVIDENCE
FOR THE RESURRECTION OF JESUS

The earliest written evidence is probably found in 1 Cor. 15:3–7, where Paul writes, "For I handed on to you as of first importance what I in turn had received; that Christ died for our sins in accordance with the scriptures, and that he was buried, and that he was raised on the third day in accordance with the scriptures." Paul's preaching in Corinth can be dated with some confidence. He stayed in Corinth for "a year and six months" (Acts 18:11) until "when Gallio was proconsul of Achaia, the Jews made a united attack on Paul and brought him before the tribunal" (v. 12). An inscription found in Delphi in 1905 makes Gallio, brother of the philosopher Seneca, proconsul in 51 C.E. As Paul stayed there "for a considerable time" (v. 18) he must have preached the resurrection about 50 C.E. or earlier, having received teaching for his belief up to ten years previously from witnesses, that is, as few as five to seven years or so after the death of Jesus, which was in about 33–35 C.E. The Gospels were written, using available documents and oral traditions, some twenty to forty years later than 52–54 C.E., the date when Paul wrote this letter to Corinth.

Paul's phrases "in accordance with the scriptures" prompts an attempt to identify these scriptures, which would have been in the Old Testament. The main candidate for the origin of the phrase, "Christ died for our sins," is Isa. 52:13–53:12. Verses 4 and 5 of chapter 53 read, "[S]urely he has borne our infirmities and carried our diseases . . . he was wounded for our transgressions, crushed for our iniquities, upon him was the punishment that made us whole." In verse 6 we read, "the Lord has laid on him the iniquity of us all," and in verse 12 "he bore the sin of many."

The Old Testament scripture reference for the raising on the third day is not so confidently identified, the only explicit reference being Hosea 6:1–2: "[the Lord] has struck down, and he will bind us up, after two days he will revive us; on the third day he will raise us up, that we may live before him," which the Fathers of the Early Church chose as the reference. The story of Jonah has been taken as allegorical evidence (Jon. 1:7): "Jonah was in the belly of the fish for three days and three nights." The equivalence of this period and "the third day" or "after three days" has several parallels in the Bible. Jesus refused a "sign" to the scribes and Pharisees, saying, "An evil and adulterous generation asks for a sign, but no sign will be given to it except the sign of the prophet Jonah" (Matt. 12:39). The use of the phrase "in accordance with the Scriptures" found in the Nicene Creed relates primarily to the New Testament and is based on a number of references.

Paul continues his orally received tradition with a list of appearances—to Peter, the Twelve, over 500 at one time, James, all the apostles, and finally Paul himself. Strangely Paul does not mention the women who, in the Gospels, are the first to see the empty tomb. According to Mark 16:1–6 they are Mary Magdalene, Mary the mother of James, and Salome. In John 20:1–2 and in the longer ending of Mark (16:9), it is Mary Magdalene alone. Luke (24:1–10) has "Mary Magdalene, Joanna and Mary the mother of James and the other women," and Matthew (28:1) has "Mary Magdalene and the other Mary." These differences between the Four Gospels are typical of the difficulties in drawing up a consistent series of events in relation to the burial, resurrection, and subsequent appearances of Jesus.

John 20:1–18 tells how "early on the first day of the week, while it was still dark, Mary Magdalene came to the tomb and saw that the stone had been removed from the tomb." She ran and told Peter and John, who saw the linen wrappings and the wrapping about the head of Jesus rolled up and in a place by itself. The disciples returned to their homes. Mary, weeping, saw two angels and, turning around, she saw Jesus. Thinking he was the gardener, she said, "Sir, if you have carried him away, tell me where you have laid him" and the reply, "Mary," convinced her that it was Jesus risen from the dead. He said, "Do not hold on to me, because I have not yet ascended to the Father, but go to my brothers."

Although the Bible does not mention that women at the time of Jesus could not bear witness in a court of law in Palestine, this is believed to be the case. There is reason to believe, however, that in Mesopotamia wives and widows throughout history appeared in court as plaintiffs, defendants, and witnesses. The Bible also does not say that women had the right to sign documents, but Israelite seals and seal impressions have been found bearing women's names, and so, as in Mesopotamia and Egypt, women did have the right to sign documents.

The significance of this has often been raised in relation to the value of the evidence of the women who were the first witnesses of the resurrection and the appearances of Jesus. It is not used today as an argument against the women's reliability as witnesses. Quite the reverse.

The fact that the women feature so prominently in the resurrection stories is claimed to be evidence of the truth of the story. It is arguable that the technical inadmissibility of women's evidence in a court of law would have influenced the attitude to women's evidence outside a court of law. That would be possible today in our society, and if it were true in New Testament times, it would then have been most unlikely that Jews wishing to make up a story would choose women to provide the evidence. On the other hand, if the women were actually there, then the use of their evidence could not very well have been avoided.

The inadmissibility of women's evidence can be contrasted with the tradition in Talmud and Midrash that Jewish women were generally considered to be "more steadfast in righteousness" than men, and truthfulness of reporting is an aspect of righteousness. This would argue even more strongly for the reliability of the witness of the women.

Matthew, Mark, and Luke are careful to note that two or more of the women watched Joseph of Arimathea roll a great stone, assisted by Nicodemus (John 19:39) and maybe others, to seal the tomb. There would then seem to be little doubt that they knew where the tomb was. Their apprehension concerning the need to roll back the stone while visiting the tomb early on Sunday morning is mentioned in Mark 16:3, but when they arrived they found that it had already been rolled away (Mark 16:4, Luke 24:2). In Mark they see a young man in the tomb, who says, "Do not be alarmed.... [Jesus] has been raised." In Luke two men in dazzling clothes say, "He has risen." Matthew alone reports that there was a great earthquake and an angel came and rolled away the stone and told the two Marys, "Do not be afraid. . . . Jesus has been raised." Those who prefer the Mark version, which seems to be the more reliable, may feel that the unidentified young man moved the stone. His final words, "He is going ahead of you to Galilee; there you will see him, just as he told you," implies that he overheard the words of Jesus on the Mount of Olives, "I will go before you to Galilee" (Mark 14:28). After Jesus was arrested all the disciples left him, but there was a young man wearing nothing but a linen cloth who had followed Jesus and whom the arresting party tried to hold. He left his clothes and escaped naked (Mark 14:51–52). Was he the person who spoke to and frightened the women early on Sunday morning?

Since, according to John 19:39, Joseph of Arimathea was assisted by Nicodemus in rolling the stone to seal the tomb, it is very unlikely that this young man alone could move the stone; there would still have been a need to find other strong men. Matthew 27:62–66 tells of guards provided by the Pharisees, who may have removed the stone, for whatever reason. These guards found the tomb empty and returned to Jerusalem (Matt. 28:11–15). They were bribed to say that the disciples stole the body while they slept, in spite of the danger to them of admitting that they slept. They were told by the priests and elders "we will . . . keep you out of trouble." "This story," says Matthew, "is still told among the Jews to this day."

Post-Resurrection Appearances of Jesus

The evidence in 1 Cor. 15:3–7 of the tradition received by Paul gives a list of appearances. This list, omitting the role of the women, has no more than a limited amount of support from the Gospels. In John 20:1–7, Peter visits the empty tomb with another disciple, but does not see Jesus until later. After the women, the next appearance in Mark is to two walking in the country, as recorded in the longer ending, (16:12). That is readily identified as the two on the way to Emmaus (Luke 24:13–32). They did not recognize Jesus until he broke bread with them—had they been then at the Last Supper? This is followed in Luke by a return to Jerusalem where, later on Sunday evening (v. 36), Jesus himself stood among the eleven, plus some others, and asked for food. This could be the event in Mark 16:14 when he appeared to the eleven as they sat at table. John's account (John 20:19–25), noting that the doors were locked for fear of the Jews, tells of the absence of Thomas, who could not believe without seeing Jesus. A week later (John 20:26), Jesus again came in through closed doors and this time Thomas was there. He was invited to see and touch the scars of Jesus, and was convinced of the resurrection.

Paul's reference to "more than five hundred brothers and sisters at one time" is unique, and the appearance to James is ambiguous as there are three—James the son of Zebedee, James the son of Alpheus (Matt. 10:2–3), and James the brother of Jesus. He may have been the James noted in John 21:2 together with Peter, Thomas, Nathanael, and the two sons of Zebedee and Salome—James and John. There are several appearances to "the apostles," including John 21:1, and "the third time that Jesus appeared to the disciples after he was raised from the dead" (John 21:14). Matthew also reports meetings with the eleven disciples (Matt. 28:16), and on a separate occasion (v. 18).

Apart from the evidence relating to the list given by Paul in 1 Corinthians 15, there are many other references in the New Testament to the resurrection, including all the letters of Paul except Philemon. No explicit reference is made in Hebrews, James, 2 Peter, the three letters of John, and Jude. There is, however, frequent recognition of the believed effects of the resurrection, particularly the gift of eternal life, throughout the New Testament both within and outside the Gospels.

The appearance to Paul noted in 1 Corinthians 15, possibly referred to in 2 Cor. 12:2–4, is identified with the journey of Saul (as Paul was first known to the Church) on the way to Damascus (recorded three times in Acts, 9:1–8, 22:6–11, 26:12–19, with typical variations of details such as any story might acquire on repetition). This appearance is different from the events in the later so-called Gospels in that it is associated with a brilliant light that temporarily blinds Saul, and there is the sound of a voice telling him to go to the Gentiles. Paul writes with conviction that he encountered the risen Jesus in person. Passages in Gal. 1:11–12 and 1:15–16 seem to refer to the same event.

If all the references to the resurrection had been closely coordinated so that there were no apparent contradictions or ambiguities, skeptics would have asserted that that the records had been edited to an extent that made them unreliable. The records as they stand have a convincing genuineness, with differences that are almost entirely understandable, bearing in mind the variety of experiences under conditions of great stress and surprise. There are, in nearly every case, time intervals of at least twenty-five years before these records were set down in writing, based no doubt on the usually reliable oral tradition. A clear-cut sequence of events cannot be deduced, nor can confident estimates be made of the reliability of key elements in the records. In particular, there are, in the New Testament canon, no explicit claims that somebody witnessed the resurrection itself. Such claims exist in the "gospel" writings that were rejected, often because of the fantastic details they describe. Little can be deduced concerning the nature of the risen body of Jesus. It is certainly not like a normal material body since he appears and disappears, passes through locked doors, and on occasions seems to be not readily recognizable.

EVIDENCE FROM THE CONVINCED DISCIPLES

John reports that the eleven disciples met on the first day of the week behind locked doors "for fear of the Jews" (John 20:19–25). Jesus appeared to them and said, "Peace be with you." He showed his hands and his side, and the disciples rejoiced, and received the Holy Spirit, which they had been told to await (Acts 1:8). Where they lived for the next forty days before the farewell "Ascension" of Jesus from Mount Olivet near Jerusalem (Acts 1:3–12) is not entirely clear. They appear to have spent time at Bethany and Galilee, and visited Jerusalem, where they eventually assembled. Peter spoke to 120 believers (Acts 1:15–26) and told of the need for an apostle to replace Judas, one who was a witness to the resurrection. They cast lots and appointed Matthias, mentioned only here.

There follows the remarkable story of Pentecost, after which the disciples and others declared openly in Jerusalem the recent events. Peter boldly preached to a crowd of devout Jews, "[Y]ou crucified [Jesus] . . . but God raised him up . . . and of that all of us are witnesses." He expounded the Old Testament passages that had been fulfilled and called to them to "repent, and be baptized every one of you in the name of Jesus Christ so that your sins may be forgiven; and you will receive the gift of the Holy Spirit." The reported result was the baptism of about 3,000 people (Acts 2:5–41).

The belief in the Early Church that the end of the world was imminent stems from Jesus' reported sayings, such as, "Truly I tell you, this generation will not pass away until all these things have taken place"

(Mark 13:30), "things" set out in verses 24–25. The belief of the Church in the resurrection gave particular significance to a firm belief in the *parousia,* the (second) coming of the Son of man "at the end of the age" (Matt. 13:40, 24:27). That belief is then itself evidence of belief in the resurrection.

There is no need to argue about the reliability of the details of the resurrection experience for the one certainty is that there was a rapid expansion of the number of believers. The preaching was extended to other places outside Palestine, and soon non-Jews were accepted into the community. The very existence of the Christian Church today is the firmest evidence of the resurrection, and the continuing experience of individual believers bears witness to the power of belief in the resurrection and the gifts of the Holy Spirit.

CHAPTER 14

Miracles

When a remarkable happening is observed and cannot be explained, age-old beliefs ascribe the cause to an intervention or regular action by God. It is called a "miracle" (Greek *dunameis*, "mighty works," "acts of power"). It is sometimes referred to as a "wonder," that is, it cannot be explained, and a "sign," that is, it is a sign from God, with a significance that is not always self-evident. In the New Testament, wonders (Greek *terata*) are always linked with signs (Greek *semeia*) in a single phrase.

Biblical miracles appear to be contrary to regularly observed processes of nature, that is, contrary to what is known of nature, contrary therefore to contemporary science. The rainbow is a good example. When it was first observed, humans were unable to explain it, and it came to be recognized as a "sign" that God would not again flood the world. It is now explained by physics as a "natural" phenomenon. It is therefore no longer called a miracle, although its beauty and appropriate appearance when rain is followed by sunshine still makes it a "wonder" of nature.

Science deals with the observed, that is, with the known and the possible. It can say nothing about impossibilities. The development of quantum theory leads to predictions of probabilities, so the most that science can say is that something that is adequately understood might be highly improbable or, on the other hand, has a very high probability of always happening. When faced with an unusual event or, better, a series of similar unusual events, the correct action of scientists is to record as carefully as possible the details of the events and then try to find an explanation in terms of existing theories. If the evidence for such an unusual event is sufficiently strong, it may indicate that some theory or theories may need smaller or larger corrections, or an entirely new theory has to be proposed. A single event, not expected to be repeated, does not lend itself readily to that procedure. Scientists can then shelve it away for future consideration and be under no pressure to take the matter further. They may express a belief that the observations were most unlikely to be reliable, but the important thing to recognize is that we are talking about beliefs, some based on scientists' knowledge of relevant science, others arising from direct observation or experience, or beliefs arising from interpretation of the record of an event, for example, in the Bible.

It is at this point that it is necessary to ask the question, "Is it important to decide which side to take?" That will bring out the prejudices of the two sides, of which the most difficult and sometimes prominent is the decision to take the Bible literally, and in particular the New Testament. Several types of miracles are recorded there, some apparently in conflict with well-established experience, such as walking on the water. Many involve medical events and, uniquely, the resurrection.

The evidence for Jesus walking on the water is found to be open to alternative translations. There are small differences in the Greek: "on the lake" in Matt. 14:25 is *epi ten thalassan*, but in Matt. 25: 26 as in Mark 6:48, and in the curiously parallel story in John 6:19, the Greek is *epi tes thalasses*. This leads some commentators to suggest that the intended meaning is "by the lake," that is, on the shore. Against this suggestion is the clear statement in Matt. 14:24 that "the boat, battered by the waves, was far from the land," with the possibility that he walked on the sea from the boat, rather than landed from the boat and walked on the seashore. We might reasonably declare that the evidence is insufficiently reliable for us to decide which translation and meaning to adopt. That may be enough to determine that it is not an important enough belief to make us take sides in the discussion of this apparent "miracle."

Theologians and most Christian believers often assign considerable importance to what they are accustomed to call miracles, of which the resurrection of Jesus has the central place, together with many reports of healing miracles. There are some opportunities, even if only a few, for subtle, difficult-to-understand events that are compatible with the underlying theories of physics as known at present. There is the further possibility of the discovery of new and even more subtle theories in the future. More particularly in relation to the resurrection of Jesus, there may be a need to recognize that some events are not able to be totally subsumed under falsifiable physical theories. Belief in miracles is then set against the beliefs of some scientists that enough is known of the theories of physics to deny the possibility of physical miracles. This implies that they believe that all events can in principle be understood as physical, but many people are not convinced that this is so. It is one belief set against another belief, for the scientists can never prove that claimed miracles are impossible. They may on reflection prefer to say that miracles are highly improbable, and many religious people would accept that.

The most important question remains: "Can we trust the evidence in the Bible?" We have already noted that the Hebrews loved stories and it is important to identify the purpose of a story and avoid a literal interpretation. The increasing number of stories of the miracles of Jesus in later writings may indicate a tendency to exaggerate or elaborate in order to provide further points for teaching spiritual matters.

It is well known that Paul in his epistles, the earliest writings in the New Testament, makes no mention of miracles other than the resurrection. Some stories in the earliest Gospel, Mark, are provided with miracles in Luke. For example, the cutting off of the ear of the high priest's servant (Mark 14:47) leads to miraculous healing in Luke (Luke 22:51). The Virgin Birth is in Luke (1:27, 34) but not in Mark—if true and known to Mark, why should he omit it? In John there are added miracles, for example, the raising of Lazarus (11:43–44) and water turned into wine (2:9).

It is not difficult to interpret these miracle stories as powerful means to impress the main points of the stories. In particular, the turning of water into wine has metaphorical links to the Last Supper, and the Holy Communion of today. Other miracles illustrate or introduce sayings of Jesus. The raising of Lazarus (John 11:25) links to "I am the resurrection and the life." The cure of the man blind from birth (John 9:1–7) is accompanied by "I am the Light of the World." The teaching of spiritual truths by means of miracle stories does not require belief in the literal truth of the stories. As evidence for miraculous events they are not all totally convincing.

Some Christians believe, in relation to miracles, that God is omnipotent and can do anything. It is important to recognize that God's omnipotence does not mean that he can do the impossible, nor can he do evil. He cannot contradict himself, for example, by breaking his own "laws of the universe," whatever we understand by these.

Jewish thinkers are faced with the apparent divine silence during the Holocaust. Some have suggested that in the act of Creation the all-powerful God had to contract (*Tsimtsum* or *Tzimtzum*) and withdraw into himself to make room for the physical world. This idea is close to that of a Kenotic Creation (p. 124), parallel to the Kenotic Incarnation (pp. 124, 140).

CHAPTER 15

Suffering

The Problem, Omnipotent God and God of Love

SUFFERING has long been a deep theological problem for those who believe that God is both omnipotent and a God of Love. The question is usually stated as, "If God is omnipotent and loving, why does he not prevent suffering?" Most people would see little or no connection between science and suffering, apart from blaming science for those applications in technology that lead to suffering, although they would readily agree that medical science has as a principal aim the alleviation of suffering. I shall consider the implications of science for the theology of suffering and the relation of suffering to human sin.

Believers in God as Creator recognize that he must be a God of order. The laws of physics explain the physical and geological evolution of the universe, and much of biological evolution. Minute changes in the magnitudes of the forces of physics would make enormous differences to the physical processes, so much so that if God chose to alter these forces, in order to effect a range of miracles of healing, our present understanding would lead us to say that it is almost certain that the universe as we know it would cease to exist. The "Anthropic Principle," (p. 66), considers this in relation to evolution.

Most believers would find it easier to question what is meant by God's omnipotence than to doubt his love. It has always been recognized that God's omnipotence cannot mean that he has the power to contradict himself—he cannot do an evil act; he cannot wantonly cause suffering; nor can he ignore suffering that he is able to remove. Some believe that God does indeed inflict suffering in order to achieve a greater good, if not in this life then in the life to come. There has been much powerful writing with this in mind, with room left for the acknowledgment of associated mystery, and paradox, but increasingly it is found to be deeply dissatisfying for people who are suffering.

It is commonly believed that God can and does intervene in the order of the universe. This is taken by many to include miraculous events, possibly without contradicting the known underlying laws of physics. This belief is sometimes closely connected with the extraordinary assumption that God controls every single event within the universe, an assumption that stretches the credulity of many people today. It also appears to offend against free will, and makes the problem of suffering even more acute. Belief in evolution under God's forces of physics, and the rich potential of chance, reduces the unimaginable multiplicity and complexity of such "hands on" acts of providence. The laws of physics thus reduce some of the difficulties in forms of belief in providence that have had a long history.

ORDER LEADS TO SUFFERING, LIMITS GOD'S ABILITY TO INTERVENE

The belief that creation has taken place and continues to take place by means of evolution removes another long-standing belief, still remarkably prevalent in sermons and writings today, namely that all suffering is the result of human sin, with the whole of creation affected by sin. Some suffering is certainly caused by human actions, but the suffering in natural disasters, such as earthquakes and volcanoes, cannot possibly be caused by humans. These natural disasters are part of continuing geological evolution, which was necessary to create the conditions suitable for life. Biological evolution is by numerous cycles of birth, survival, procreation, and physical death, and these, with all the suffering they involve, including the suffering of animals, are likewise not the result of human sin.

Most scientists agree that divine intervention to avoid suffering would involve a direct violation of the laws of physics, and would produce such a measure of disorder in the universe, not only locally but distant in space and time, that the order in the universe would be destroyed, and "the Anthropic Principle" would cease to operate. Put another way, God would have contradicted himself. With the possible exception of rare miracles, God seems to be unable to intervene on a grand scale to reduce the suffering in the world. It has been suggested that it is possible that in the act of Creation of an ordered universe, God deliberately limited his ability to intervene and disturb the order. Such a self-limitation or "emptying" implies a *Kenotic* Creation, within which God would not be able to intervene to prevent physical suffering. A similar Rabbinic thought, known as *Tzimtzum* (= contraction), was taught by Isaac ben Solomon Luria (1534–72) living in Syria, as the basic doctrine of Lurianic Kabbala, a form of esoteric mysticism. God is believed to have withdrawn (= *tzimtzum*) his overwhelming divine light from a region of space in order to make room for the physical universe. Luria's influence was far-reaching, especially in the eighteenth-century Hasidic movement. However, intervention may be possible by other means than through the natural order that has been deduced from the discoveries of science, discoveries that can be seen as part only of God's revelation of what he is like. For example, direct benevolent influences on minds cannot be ruled out, if it is accepted that minds are not wholly explicable as arising from physical processes in the human brain.

In the Incarnation, the New Creation, there was believed to be a parallel self-limitation, or emptying, by Jesus, "who, though he was in the form of God, did not regard equality with God as something to be exploited, but emptied himself, taking the form of a slave, being born in human likeness. And being found in human form, he humbled himself and became obedient to the point of death—even death on a cross" (Phil. 2:6–8). Some begin to feel that God suffers whenever humankind suffers.

Such a thought raises a number of questions of which the most important, as asked by Leibnitz, is probably, "Is this the best of all possible universes?" Recognition of the self-limitation of the Creator resolves part of the problem of suffering in our universe, but leaves us with this tantalizing question, answered by Leibnitz in the positive. It is easy to imagine some of the natural events that we would like to change, in order to make this a better universe. That is, however, a far cry from thinking through all the consequences, including the changing of both nature's laws and the magnitudes of their physical constants, while still allowing evolution to the kind of human that we would like to be. We do not know what would be the best of all possible universes, and if we did we would not know how to prescribe for its evolution.

WHAT ARE THE ADVANTAGES OF ORDER IN THE UNIVERSE?

A natural question is, "What are the advantages of order in Creation if it inevitably leads to the problem of suffering?" The first realization is that order is essential, together with chance, in the evolution of the universe. It must have been one of God's prime considerations to create the forces of physics with prescient precision, in order to evolve sentient and rational humans, able to become theologians and scientists.

The next realization is that order is essential to make free will a genuine possibility. We choose between "this with these consequences" and "that with those consequences," believing that the subsequent events in nature will be consistent with the order in our past experience. So order underlies free will, and of course free will leads to good and evil.

Order is also recognized as essential to provide trustworthiness, reliability, constancy, steadfastness in God's Creation. These are characteristic underlying prerequisite factors of love, deeper than many other factors, known both in our love for each other, and in trust in a loving God.

These three advantages of order in Creation are types of the love of the Creator. True love is unlimited; there is a type of this in the unlimited sphere of spatial, temporal, and emergent evolution provided by the love of the Creator. True love is also vulnerable, and this is revealed in the free will made possible by order, which causes suffering to humans when they choose wrong rather than right, with consequent suffering to God. In spite of the assurance of trustworthiness and constancy that stem from order, the love of humans with free will has its perils and its problems and the same characteristics are seen in the true and empathetic love of the Creator.

CONCLUSIONS FOR BELIEF ABOUT SUFFERING

Science and some theological insights lead us to these conclusions;

1. The physical universe appears to be based on inviolate order.

2. Throughout Creation, God is self-limited, submitting to his own established order, and he cannot therefore intervene to prevent all physical suffering. (St. Paul tells us that, in the New Creation, the divine-incarnate Jesus was self-limited.)

3. Physical miracles cannot be said by scientists to be impossible; if they happen they must be relatively rare.

4. Some, but not all, suffering is the result of human ignorance or sin. Suffering and physical death as essential parts of the course of evolution, and arising from today's natural disasters, cannot be the result of human sin.

5. The advantages of order in Creation include the provision of means for evolution, the guarantee of free will, and prerequisites of love. They are evidence of the love of God.

PERSONAL EXPERIENCE

In early 1997 I was diagnosed with cancer of the lymphatic system (Hodgkin's disease) and the vicar called to see me. He was not interested in the symptoms, the tests or the treatment, but wanted to know how I had taken the news. It was near Easter and I had been singing, "This is the day that the Lord has made, let us rejoice and be glad in it" (Ps. 118:24). I had rewritten it to use as a kind of mantra: "This is the way that the World is made, let us rejoice and be glad in it." This arose from the thoughts given above and the vicar knew that I had accepted what had happened, and that I had peace and trust and even a little excitement in my heart. Six months of distressing chemotherapy, and good care from my wife, a retired general practitioner, resulted in a steady recovery, in spite of an underlying problem with my heart. I most certainly rejoice and am glad that the world is made the way it is, with the assurance of God's presence in this life and the promise of life after death.

In January 2005, pneumonia, treated in hospital, evoked the same optimistic trust.

NATURAL DISASTERS

There is clear evidence of several types of natural disasters. One type is an event with no evidence of human involvement in the cause, for example, the earthquake and tsunami in the Indian Ocean in December 2004, with 300,000 killed and millions made homeless. A second type is an event with evidence of human involvement in its cause, for example, widespread floods, droughts, and high winds, in part associated with deforestation and global warming. Because humans are closely involved, it is not surprising that humans are sometimes blamed, with the readily associated belief that the "act of God" is a punishment for human sins. This reflects rather directly what is believed to be the nature of God, frequently referred to in the Old Testament in the history of the Israelites, for example, "Vengeance is mine" (Deut. 32:35), and also in a number of New Testament passages, including the reported words of Jesus, Luke 13:2–5, "Unless you repent you will all perish just as they did." It is difficult to accept that this belief relates persuasively to the way God loves the world, sending his only Son to save the world by the Incarnation, and the acts, death, and resurrection of Jesus.

The first type is sometimes referred to as an "act of God," as if God planned and controlled it. There is evidence from geology that the event is part of the way the world is made, and the world is still evolving. As seen already, it appears that God does not, and cannot, intervene to prevent or control such events. It would seem that he limited his ability to intervene when he began creating the physical world, *Kenotic Creation*, in order not to contradict his own laws of physics.

The second type is more open to debate. The extent of the human involvement is often disputed, for example, in global warming. Attempts are sometimes made to reduce known human factors, such as "greenhouse" gases from carbon fuels that lead to global warming, but some countries stubbornly refuse to accept scientific explanations and change their lifestyles.

Recently, steps have been taken to give global and local warnings of the first type of events. Tsunami waves, several meters high, travel at 500 m.p.h. and radio warnings can therefore give an hour's warning for countries 500 miles from the initial disturbance. This has been introduced in Japan and in the Pacific and work is beginning for the Indian Ocean. Such systems can save some lives, but destruction and suffering remain.

Volcanoes have known locations but largely unknown times of eruption. Humans can protect themselves by choosing where to live to avoid volcanoes. The danger of volcanoes is revealed by a study of the catastrophic mass extinction 250 million years ago (p. 77). Intense volcanic activity polluted the atmosphere with toxic gases and "greenhouse" gases, producing excessive global warming and a reduction of atmospheric oxygen from 21 to 16 percent, with fatal consequences.

Some believe that "acts of God" serve to show the role of love in the way he and his creatures respond to consequential suffering. Such a belief does not come readily to many people. A more common belief is that suffering from "acts of God" will be canceled by the good things to be experienced in heaven.

We can still respond with "This is the way the world is made," and some individuals in the event can continue, "Let us rejoice and be glad in it," but for those most affected we can but continue, "Lord have mercy."

There is a deep conviction among both Christians and believers in other religions that God does in some way show his providential love and care for his creation. This may be through the minds of humans who are aware of a religious experience and of their common humanity and who respond, as the hands and feet of providence, with great love and care for victims.

CHAPTER 16

Incarnation and Atonement

INTRODUCTION

INCARNATION and Atonement belong together. Atonement is the aim, and Incarnation the means. Incarnation means literally "embodying in flesh" (Latin *carnis*, genitive of *caro*, "flesh") and in Christian belief refers to the event in which Jesus, the "Son of God," was born to a human mother. The word *Incarnation* does not occur in the Bible, but is most explicitly covered by John 1:14: "the Word became flesh and lived among us, and we have seen his glory, the glory as of a father's only Son, full of grace and truth." Atonement as a belief of Christians is defined in one dictionary as "the reconciliation of God and humans by means of the Incarnation and death of Christ." By *reconciliation* is meant "restoration to friendship or union." In biblical terms, what broke that friendship or union was sin. Sin leads to estrangement from God. Atonement then means forgiveness of a repentant sinner and a new relationship with God.

The evidence for the events of Incarnation and Atonement is interrelated, and the evidence for interpretations and explanations has much in common. Historical evidence for belief in the events of both Incarnation and Atonement is found in the Bible and is based on sayings and on personal experiences. Such reports of personal experiences will be convincing to an inquirer only if relevant parallels to the experience of others can be identified within the experience of the inquirer. The evidence for explanations and interpretations stems from reasoning found in the Bible, and depends also on the work of theologians, particularly during the first five centuries after Christ. This work continues today.

The language and images in which experiences are described are important in attempting to evaluate the evidence for the Atonement as an event, and they will have considerable influence in the development of doctrinal explanations. The Atonement in the New Testament is vividly expressed in the phrase, "Christ died for our sins," as written, for example, by Paul in 1 Cor. 15:3: "for I handed on to you as of first importance what I in turn had received, that Christ died for our sins." We need to find out what this meant to the writer, and to the readers and hearers, at the time when it was written. Then there is a need to consider what it means for present-day believers and seekers.

THE JEWISH DAY OF ATONEMENT

An important Jewish annual festival is the Day of Atonement, Yom Kippur. This has been, since the fourth century B.C.E., a forefront belief of Jews, and therefore a vital part of the upbringing of Jesus and his disciples, and also of Paul. Yom Kippur was held at the end of a ten-day penitential period, the first day of which was the Jewish civil New Year. The first Bible reference is in Leviticus 16, for example, verse 30, "for on this day atonement shall be made for you to cleanse you from all your sins." Further details are found in Lev. 23:27–32, 25:9, and Num. 29:7–11. Before the destruction of the Temple in 70 C.E., the key point in this Atonement was in sacrifices for the expiation, "covering over" or "taking away," of sins, invoking God's forgiveness. There is also an element of intended "propitiation," the appeasing of a displeased or angry God (Exod. 32:10). The High Priest placed his hands upon a goat (Lev. 16:21) as he confessed and transferred the real or deliberate sins of the people. The goat, as substitute, was then taken into the wilderness to die. According to later accounts, when a wilderness was not nearby, the goat was thrown over a precipice. This "scapegoat" bore the blame for other sins that could not be expiated by making amends. In the same ritual another goat was sacrificed, for unwitting or inadvertent sins such as failure in carrying out prescribed rituals. Nowadays, Jews spend the Day of Atonement in fasting, prayer, and confession.

THE NEW TESTAMENT ACCOUNTS
OF THE ATONEMENT

It was instructive for me to read through the New Testament and list all the verses relating directly or indirectly to the Incarnation and to the Atonement. These, as expected, show the influence of contemporary beliefs among the Jews. In the early history of the Church, recorded in the Acts of the Apostles, salvation is mainly related to the whole experience of Jesus, as in Acts 5:31: "God exalted him at his right hand as Leader and Savior, so that he might give repentance to Israel and forgiveness of sins." Emphasis was on "telling the good news about Jesus and the resurrection" (Acts 17:18), but later the focal point was seen as his death, as in Acts 20:28, "keep watch over yourselves . . . to shepherd the church of God, that he obtained with the blood of his own son."

The most frequent New Testament image is of Christ's sacrifice, as in 1 Cor. 5:7, "for our Paschal lamb, Christ, has been sacrificed," which was "once for all" (Heb. 7:27). The image of "redemption" or "ransoming" is used in the Old Testament for divine activity in rescuing Israel from material perils and hardships. The words occur twenty-five times in the AV New Testament, arising primarily from the saying of Jesus in Mark 10:45 (= Matt. 20:28), "For the Son of Man came not to be served but to serve, and to give his life a ransom for many." Here and elsewhere sacrifice and ransom are brought together. Another image used to express atonement is "justification," being brought into a right relation with God, but not by adhering to the law of Moses since "we know that a person is justified not by the works of the law but through faith in Jesus Christ" (Gal. 2:16). The image of "reconciliation" is given in 2 Cor. 5:19, "in Christ God was reconciling the world to himself, not counting their trespasses against them." This was particularly appropriate for gentile listeners who, from the Jewish standpoint, had been considered to be enemies of God, and of the Jews, as in Rom. 5:10: "For if, while we were enemies, we were reconciled to God through the death of his Son, much more surely, having been reconciled, will we be saved by his life." There is a changed relationship between God and humans as a result of the work of Christ.

Paul brings together sacrifice, justification, and propitiation in Rom. 5:8–9: "For God proves his love for us in that while we still were sinners Christ died for us. Much more surely then, now that we have been justified by his blood, will we be saved through him from the wrath of God."

The wealth of these images bears witness to the importance of the Atonement for the early Christians. Their variety arises from the complexity of the thoughts raised concerning the relationship between God and humans. It is necessary to try to understand what is being explained, and to estimate the acceptability of the basic ideas in the days of the Early Church and also today.

REFERENCES TO ATONEMENT IN HYMNS

As noted on p. 55, hymns are evidence of the beliefs of their authors, and they influence the beliefs of those who sing them. To that extent they act as bases for belief or for reinforcement or changing of existing beliefs. In assessing the frequencies of reference to a range of topics in hymns it is found that there are uncertainties arising from the precise words selected. For *Ancient and Modern New Standard* (AMNS) two separate counts were made to check reliability, and the second count was in nearly every case somewhat larger, almost certainly caused by the acceptance of implied meanings rather than simply the occurrence of one or two particular words to identify the topic. The counts for the other two hymnbooks used more nearly equal criteria.

The Table below shows the frequencies normalized per 500 hymns for *Ancient and Modern New Standard, Common Praise* and *Mission Praise*.

The word "Redeemer" is very probably used and understood in a general sense, equivalent to "Savior" and the parallel "Salvation." Love as the implied key to Atonement is frequent in all three hymnbooks, and can be distributed among terms such as "Christ's love," "love that forgives," and "pure love." Direct references are few, for example "divine love" and "Father's love," and often retain a link to the images

TERM USED	AMNS	CP	MP
Sacrifice[a]	48	37	41
Cross or crucify[b]	47	20	34
Ransom[c]	51	22	36
Redeemer	25	37	20
Savior	71	93	90
Salvation	29	25	29
Devil or Satan	14	17	11
linked to a fight	18	8	13
Hell	17	4	11
Adam[d] and Eve[e]	6	5	4
The Mystery of Atonement	8	4	4

a   Direct, or implied by "Priest" or "blood."

b   With appeals to our emotions

c   Or "paying the price" or "redemption"

d   Both first and second

e   A reference in AMNS to the Mother of Jesus as the "second Eve" who "love's answer made which our redemption won" (hymn 360) is omitted in CP (no. 238).

already considered, for example, "sacrificial love," "redeeming love," "ransoming love." The Cross is the subject of a number of appeals to our emotions, and there are many references to "Christ died for my sins" without direct mention of the Cross or "crucify."

For the three hymnbooks there are, per 500 hymns, 319, 280, and 300 hymns referring to Atonement. It is not possible to decide whether significant differences in image frequency in these three hymnbooks arise from deliberate policy decisions about Atonement or depend on a wider range of considerations, such as perceived poetic quality. One comment is obvious, however: ransom including redemption and Redeemer is a frequent image, with an average total of 64 per 500 hymns for the three books. Hell and Christ's fight against the Devil still have a place with an average total of 41 per 500 hymns for the three books. Sacrifice is also frequently mentioned, average total 42 per 500 hymns, and the Cross has an average total of 34 per 500 hymns. The terms "Savior" and "Salvation" appear to be used in a general or neutral sense with an average total of 112 per 500 hymns. Mystery is rarely mentioned. There are several suggestions that Atonement is not a single event, but a continuing process matching the continuing sinfulness of humankind, consonant with the belief that the devil has not been totally defeated.

ATONEMENT EVENTS

For many people the most widespread and convincing evidence for the events of Atonement is the simple fact that a very large number of contemporary Jews and Gentiles declared their belief in their happening and effectiveness. This response was related to Jesus, his works, and his death and Resurrection. Of these, the event most frequently singled out was his death, as shown in the Bible references presented above. Identifying his death in terms of sacrifice made a natural link to the Jewish sacrifice on the Day of Atonement.

The immediate effect on the believers was a conviction that because they had repented and having declared their belief in the gospel of Jesus, their sins had been forgiven, and the reason for this belief must be related to the preaching of Jesus, and also the power of Jesus to heal the sick and rise from the dead.

This growing belief in the Atonement continued in spite of, or even in part because of, persecutions by the civil and religious authorities. Conflicting and complementary explanations of Atonement were common for several centuries, and continue indeed even today. However, that some atoning event had taken place through the life and death of Jesus, his Resurrection and Ascension, and the gift of the Holy Spirit, was rarely challenged and has become, together with the Incarnation, a central belief of Christians.

THE WORD (*LOGOS*)

At the heart of belief in the event of Atonement, and in attempts to explain the process, there is the belief that Christ was more than an ordinary human. In fact, he was believed to be the Word, the incarnate Son of God. The meaning of *Word* is explained in John 1:1–14:

> In the beginning was the Word [*Logos* in Greek], and the Word was with God, and the Word was God. He was in the beginning with God. All things came into being through him, and without him not one thing came into being. . . . He was in the world, and the world came into being through him; yet the world did not know him. He came to what was his own, and his own people did not accept him. But to all who received him, who believed in his name, he gave power to become children of God.

There can be no doubt that "the Word" refers to Jesus. Elsewhere in John's Gospel there is no mention of the Logos, and some believe that the Prologue, John 1:1–5, was an existing hymn of the Logos, possibly not even Christian.

John's Gospel is generally agreed to be later than the first three Gospels. The terms used are often different from the earlier way of speaking or writing and show the influence of Greek thought, as in the use of the term *Logos* in chapter 1. The word *Logos* was first used in the sixth century before Christ by the Greek philosopher Heraclitus for a divine force producing order and discernible patterns in the universe. After the fourth century B.C.E., *Logos* is used for a rational divine power identified with God. The Stoics of the time advised, "Follow where Reason [= the *Logos*] leads." In the first century C.E. the Jewish-Hellenistic philosopher Philo used *Logos* as the name of a mediating principle between God and the world, God's Word or Wisdom. In

John there is a combination of such Greek ideas and Hebrew ideas. In the Old Testament, the phrase "the word of the Lord," meaning any communication believed to have been made by God to humans, especially through a prophet, without any suggestion of a personified Word occurs nearly 400 times.

SON OF MAN AND SON OF GOD

In the AV Gospels the title "Son of man" occurs eighty-one times and is used by Jesus, and by him alone, often implying himself. The AV in Matt. 16:13 reads, "Whom do men say that I the Son of man am?" following the Greek of many ancient authorities. The RV and modern translations, following the presently accepted Greek text, read, "Who do men say that the Son of man is?" Nowhere, other than this verse in AV Matthew does Jesus explicitly claim to be the Son of man. In the AV Ezekiel is addressed by God as "son of man" eighty-seven times with no evidence of divine significance. It is translated as "O mortal" in the NRSV. Some have given emphasis to the passage in Dan. 7:13–14, in the AV translation, "I saw in the night visions, and, behold, one like the Son of man [RV reads "like unto a son of man"] came with the clouds of heaven, and came to the Ancient of Days . . . and there was given him dominion, and glory, and a kingdom . . . an everlasting dominion." The NRSV reads, "As I watched in the night visions, I saw one like a human being [a footnote gives the meaning of the Aramaic as "one like a son of man"] coming with the clouds of heaven. And he came to the Ancient One." In both translations the Son of man is evidently not a title, since the phrase is introduced by "like," and yet the mention of "clouds of heaven" brings to mind the answer of Jesus to the high priest's question, "Are you the Messiah, the Son of the Blessed One?," namely, "I am [i.e., the Son of God] and you will see the Son of Man seated at the right hand of the Power, and coming with the clouds of heaven" (Mark 14:62; see also Mark 13:26, with parallels in Matthew and Luke). It would appear that Jesus may have associated himself with the passage in Dan. 7:13–14, which is generally interpreted as a figure that signals the end of history, but the Old Testament reference could have been invoked by the Gospel writers as a "proof" text of fulfilled prophecy.

The term "Son of God" in the Old Testament appears to mean "belonging to God," as in Exod. 4:22, "Israel is my firstborn son," and in reference to a Davidic king and his successors in 2 Sam. 7:14, "I will be a father to him, and he shall be a son to me." "Son of God" occurs twenty-four times in the AV (and RV) Gospels, ten of which are in John's Gospel. Jesus is accused of saying he was the Son of God (Matt. 27:43; Mark 14:62; John 10:36, 19:7), which is declared to be blasphemy. The significance of the two different terms, Son of man and Son of God, is not clear, although Son of God appears to relate more directly to the divine origin of Jesus, and Son of man more to his humanity. In Rom. 1:4 Paul writes of the gospel concerning God's Son, "declared to be Son of God with power according to the spirit of holiness by resurrection from the dead." Paul also calls Christ "the power of God and the wisdom of God" (1 Cor. 1:24) and declares "all things have been created through him and for him. He himself is before all things, and in him all things hold together. . . . For in him all the fullness of God was pleased to dwell, and through him God was pleased to reconcile to himself all things, whether on earth or in heaven, by making peace through the blood of his cross" (Col. 1:16–17, 19–20).

Sayings of Jesus reveal what he saw as his mission, but relatively few relate to what he saw as his identity. His claim to have the ability to forgive sins was clearly demonstrated and challenged by the Jewish authorities. Jesus said to a paralyzed man, "Son, your sins are forgiven" (Mark 2:5//Matt. 9:2//Luke 5:20) to which the scribes and Pharisees responded, "Who can forgive sins but God alone?" Later (Mark 2:10) Jesus said, "But so that you may know that the Son of Man has authority on earth to forgive sins," he said to the paralytic, "I say to you, stand up, take your mat, and go to your home." To the woman leading an immoral life he said, "Your sins are forgiven" (Luke 7:48). It became the belief of the apostles, and converts such as Paul, that Jesus was more than the human son of a carpenter.

The only saying of Jesus that appears to claim that he knew himself to be God is found in John 8:58–59, "Very truly, I tell you, before Abraham was, I am. So they [the Jews] picked up stones to throw at him," for they recognized this as a usage from the Old Testament for divine identity. No parallel or similar saying is reported in the first three Gospels, and it can be argued that this is an example of John's tendency to concentrate more on perceived spiritual truths than on historical accuracy. Many of John's more difficult reported sayings appear to be derived from later beliefs of the Church.

THE MESSIAH

Roman occupation of Palestine led to an increase in the hope for and expectation of the Messiah, the promised political deliverer of Israel. In 63 B.C.E. the Roman Pompey the Great captured Jerusalem. Herod, a practicing Jew, backed by the Romans, was King of Judea (37–4 B.C.E.), and began to rebuild the Temple in 19 B.C.E. (completed 25 C.E.). Direct Roman rule of Judea was enforced in 6 C.E. Tiberius Caesar was the second emperor of Rome (14–37 C.E.). Pontius Pilate was Roman prefect of Judea (26–36 C.E.). The Jews revolted in 66 C.E. and held Jerusalem until the city was sacked, and the Temple finally destroyed, in 70 C.E.

Messiah comes from the Hebrew *mashiach*, meaning "the anointed one" (*christos* in the Greek Septuagint), and pointed to a king, a Davidic king, believed to be a ruler over Israel. The Messiah came to be linked to the Suffering Servant of Isa. 52:13–53:12, an image explicitly adopted by Jesus.

Jesus came to be regarded by some as the expected Messiah, a potential political liberator, essentially human. The Gospels record that his identity was proclaimed by angels at the time of his conception (Matt. 1:20–23) "conceived from the Holy Spirit . . . a son, Jesus, for he will save his people from their sins. . . . [T]hey shall name him Emmanuel, which means God is with us," again at his birth (Luke 2:9–14), "a Savior, who is the Messiah, the Lord," and also at his baptism by John (Mark 1:11), "my Son, the Beloved." Some believe that these are unlikely to be strictly historical statements, and were devotional inserts made many years after the events, but there is other supporting evidence. Once when Jesus healed the sick, the demons that came out shouted, "You are the Son of God!" (Luke 4:41). "But he rebuked them and would not allow them to speak, because they knew that he was the Messiah."

Later, when Jesus asked his disciples, "Who do people say that the Son of Man is?" they answered, "Some say John the Baptist, but others Elijah, and still others Jeremiah or one of the prophets." Then Jesus said, "But who do you say that I am?" Simon Peter answered, "You are the Messiah, the Son of the living God." Then Jesus said, "Blessed are you, Simon son of Jonah! For flesh and blood has not revealed this to you, but my Father in heaven. . . . He sternly ordered the disciples not to tell any one that he was the Messiah," and "From that time on, Jesus began to show his disciples that he must go to Jerusalem, and undergo great suffering . . . and be killed, and on the third day be raised" (Matt. 16:13–17, 20, 21). When he was arrested and asked by the high priest (Mark 14:61–62), "Are you the Messiah, the Son of the Blessed One?" Jesus said, "I am, and you will see the Son of Man seated at the right hand of the Power and coming with the clouds of heaven." It was this public declaration that led to his crucifixion. Messiah was linked to the concept of kingship and was misunderstood to be a claim by Jesus to be "King of the Jews" (Mark 15:12, 18, 26), rather than related to "the Kingdom of God," of which he had much to say, mostly in parables.

The Kenotic Incarnation

The title *Son of God* applied to Jesus raises the question, "Was Jesus both divine and human?" This leads to a considerable literature on the two "natures" in Jesus, much of it based on the evidence of reasoning concerning the need for both in the action of Atonement. One significant early text is often quoted, "Jesus, who, though he was in the form of God, did not regard equality with God as something to be exploited, but emptied himself, taking the form of a slave, being born in human likeness. And being found in human form, he humbled himself and became obedient to the point of death—even death on a cross" (Phil. 2:5–8). This passage, in almost classical artistic prose, is considered by some to be part of a hymn, or possibly part of a credal statement.

Evidence of this kenosis (from Greek *kenos* = empty), or self-limitation, is confirmed by the story of Jesus being tempted to use his divine power (Matt. 4:1ff.). Jesus, it has been claimed, was not aware of his own divinity, and did not use it in order to undergo all the experiences of humanity. After his death, he revealed his divine power in the Resurrection and in the Ascension. His cry from the cross, "It is finished," is better translated as "It is accomplished," for what was accomplished was his divine mission, to be fully human, to set an example, and to provide Atonement. "It is finished" is weaker; it could mean no more than "this is the end of my life."

ATTEMPTS TO EXPLAIN THE ATONEMENT

The Atonement as an event leading to the forgiving of sin is firmly believed by all Christians, but the attempts to explain what was the method of Christ's action are many, and at times strange to our present ways of thinking. This is already obvious in the New Testament, and the reasoning continued in the early Councils. Conflicting emphases were judged by the Early Church but came into the open in 1050 to 1350 and again at the time of the Reformation. I shall not enter into a detailed discussion of the many different points of view. Instead I shall consider the underlying assumptions and consider those that relate directly to present-day human experience, and those that are less likely to appeal as evidence for contemporary people.

Sacrifices

Today the image of the appeasing of an angry God by sacrifices of animals, oils, or grain is not conducive to our understanding of the Atonement, but this is not intended to rule out the importance of sacrifice as a metaphorical theme in our religious thinking. The notion of an angry God is surely un-Christian (Rom. 5:9), but the deep-rooted belief in the efficacy of Jewish sacrifices was able to be taken over without much difficulty by many of the first Christians. The need was felt to purify the ideas involved, and this was particularly evident in relation to the words of Jesus used in the consecration of the elements, "On the first day of the week, when we met to break bread" (Acts 20:7), or the Eucharist (1 Cor. 11:23–26), "the Lord...took a loaf of bread, and when he had given thanks, he broke it and said 'This is my body that is for you. Do this in remembrance of me,' and after supper said, 'This cup is the new covenant in my blood.... For as often as you eat this bread and drink the cup, you proclaim the Lord's death until he comes.'" Some Christians have taken the words "this is my body" literally and have developed the doctrine of "Transubstantiation," believing in the distinction between substance and appearance identified by Aristotle, that there is a real change in the substance of the bread and wine, perceived by the mind, without a change in appearance perceived by the senses. This was coupled with the belief that in Holy Communion the communicant is united with Christ and partakes of the sacrifice of Christ. Some are reluctant to use, in any sense, the word *sacrifice* of the Eucharist.

The Anglican Liturgy refers explicitly in the Prayer of Consecration at the Holy Communion of the *Book of Common Prayer* (1662) to Christ making on the Cross "a full, perfect and sufficient sacrifice, oblation, and satisfaction, for the sins of the whole world." This is preserved in the recent (2000) Common Worship Prayer C, where later (as also in Prayer B) there is the phrase, "we offer you through [Jesus Christ] this our sacrifice of praise" (see Heb. 13:15) and "sacrifice of thanksgiving" (see Lev. 7:12). Prayer C adds the qualifying phrase, "Although we are unworthy, through our manifold sins, to offer you any sacrifice, yet we pray that you will accept this the duty and service that we owe." Prayer F refers to "the one, perfect sacrifice of our redemption." Prayer G includes "Father, we plead with confidence his sacrifice made once for all upon the cross."

The Anglican Alternative Service Book (ASB, 1980), in its Third Eucharistic Prayer, described Christ as savior who "opened wide his arms for us on the cross; he put an end to death by dying for us." The Fourth Eucharistic Prayer followed the wording of 1662 quoted above but omitted "oblation and satisfaction." In the Second Eucharistic

Prayer the theme of Christ's sacrifice was absent. The language of penal substitution and propitiation was avoided in the ASB but the vicarious nature of sacrifice was retained.

The longstanding Christian tradition of calling the death of Jesus a sacrifice was detached from the actions of the Jewish community in the time of Jesus. After the destruction of the Temple in 70 C.E., sacrifices ceased and reference to sacrifice in Jewish liturgy necessarily required metaphorical interpretation. It is clear that use of the word *sacrifice* to refer to the life and death of Jesus can have a valuable metaphorical meaning. The word *sacrifice* is dominant in hymns (see p. 133) and liturgy, but few if any Christians think in terms of Jewish sacrifices of animals. A common parallel in preaching is that provided by soldiers, sailors, and airmen in times of war. They sacrifice, that is, give their lives willingly for a good cause, the community they love. There are also many examples of caring relatives and friends who dedicate their lives to the service of others, sacrificing their material opportunities for more spiritually rewarding occupations. The word *sacrifice* is so deeply embedded in the experiences of humans that it will surely continue to be used for the action of Jesus in setting his face toward Jerusalem, knowing what awaited him there. There is no suggestion by Jesus that he is propitiating an angry Father.

Sacrifices were, of course, important features in many religions. At Lystra Paul healed a cripple (Acts 14:8–18) and the response was "The gods have come down to us in human form!" The priest of the temple of Zeus "brought oxen and garlands to the gates; he and the crowds wanted to offer sacrifice." Paul and Barnabas tore their clothes and rushed into the crowd saying, "We are mortals, just like you," and "they scarcely restrained the crowds from offering sacrifice to them." This sacrifice would not have been to "appease an angry God" but rather to express their respect and awe for divinity.

The Latin word *sacrificium* literally means "something made sacred," but is used to translate the Greek *thusia* and the Hebrew *zebah,* which mean "slaughter."

Redemption and Ransom

The word *redemption* is derived from the buying back of something that formerly belonged to the purchaser, for example, a slave, and has the same root in Greek as the word *ransom*. As an explanation of what happens in the Atonement it was early realized that ransom raises the questions: (1) What is bought back for the sinner?; (2) From whom?; and (3) What is the ransom that is paid? What is bought back is the sense of freedom from the slavery of sin, and this is related to the belief in the creation of man as "morally perfect," a state from which, the Bible tells us, he fell at the first sin. The ransom is considered to be the life of Jesus, paid to the Devil, but Anselm (1033–1109) asked, "Why should we accept that the Devil has any legal right over against the infinite Creator?'

In the evolution of man, belief in original perfection and the Fall is difficult to retain, and hence the doctrine of "Original Sin" that is passed down through the ages, as if it is a genetic defect, is suspect. Over many generations, humans gradually became aware of their individual identity, and the similar identities of others. They experienced actions of other humans that caused offense. They experienced regret, especially when they themselves recognized in others what it was like to be offended. The expression of sorrow is linked to man-to-man confession and apology, and perhaps reparation to a fellow human. When an awareness of the need for a personal Creator God had been developed, there was developed in parallel the sense of need to confess the offense to God, ask his forgiveness, and offer something in reparation. The intensity of this need was related to the development of the human view of the image of God the Creator, an image discovered and revealed in terms of what it was to be human at humankind's very best. The belief in the omnipotence, omniscience, and infinite love of God, and his omnipresence, included the belief that humans must have initially been made perfect. By the time humans felt able to say, "Humans were made in the image of God," it was natural to try to explain how sin and forgiveness entered human experience, hence the Genesis stories.

Evolution as a fact appears to be certain, but the ways in which it comes about are not completely understood. The most important process is generally agreed to be "survival of the fittest," both within a species and between species. The "fittest" are self-evidently "the fittest to survive." This process requires actions that border on the moral distinctions by humans between right and wrong. Some "unfit" humans are preserved by mercy and love. The very processes of evolution are sometimes used to blame the Creator for the presence of sin and suffering among his creatures. The importance of free will then becomes paramount, but it is generally agreed that competition between individuals is one of the most potent actions leading to sin, and the cause of much suffering by humans, as well as by animals.

Experience of sin is common to all humans, and there must be very few who feel that there is never a need to be reconciled to the victim of the sin, even to God himself. Just how sacrifices to God came to be chosen as the right way to restore the God-human relationship is a matter of long-standing debate. And how sacrifices effected "atonement" was also answered in a variety of ways, including propitiation and expiation. In this context arose the idea of "ransom" or "redemption," based on the contemporary human experience of slavery and the opportunity to be granted freedom. The development of belief in Satan or the Devil, probably accentuated by the Exile in Babylon, led to the crude belief that sinning was selling or pawning one's soul to the Devil. Forgiveness and restoration of relationships, with freedom from sin, could then be achieved, so some believed that by paying a ransom to the Devil, one could redeem one's pledge. The cost of animal sacrifices could be seen as a ransom to the Devil, extending and confusing the meaning of sacrifices to God. In dwelling on the work of Christ, and in the belief that his life and death was at the heart of the Atonement, the idea of a ransom paid by Christ to the Devil was seen in terms of the giving of his life and the surrender of his soul.

This idea of ransom was popular in the Early Church, possibly because of the saying that occurs only in Mark 10:45 (= Matt. 20:28), "For the Son of Man came not to be served but to serve, and to give his life a ransom for many." This is the only saying of Jesus that appears to attempt an explanation of the Atonement, and its authenticity has been questioned. The idea of ransom was held until Anselm's doctrine of "satisfaction" in the eleventh century. In a popular subplot God was believed to have outwitted the Devil. Gregory of Nyssa (331–395 C.E.) wrote of "Deity hidden under the veil of our nature, that so, as with ravenous fish, the hook of the Deity might be gulped down along with the bait of the flesh." Augustine used the strange imagery of Christ "holding out his cross to the Devil like a mouse trap, and, as a bait, set on it his own blood." Such ideas are most unlikely to be attractive to seekers or believers today.

Christ's victory over the Devil is another image of the Early Church, as found in Heb. 2:14: "He himself likewise shared the same things [flesh and blood], so that through death he might destroy the one who has the power of death, that is, the devil." The belief is given emphasis in icons of eastern Christendom and holds together the death on the Cross and the perceived destruction of the power of death, the Devil, in the Resurrection. Here the defeat of the ransomer is seen as the key action in Atonement. Many today, referring to the Devil by means of metaphor, and aware of the evil still found in the world, would not accept that the Devil has been universally defeated.

It is common to refer to Jesus as our "Redeemer," the payer of a ransom, and the memory is stimulated by the stirring rendering of "I know that my Redeemer liveth" in Handel's *Messiah*. The words come from Job 19:25 (AV and NIV). Other translations use the word *vindicator* (REB and RV). NRSV reads, "For I know that my Redeemer lives," and GNB rewrites the statement as, "I know there is someone in heaven who will come at last to my defense." This GNB version is generally regarded as the closest to the meaning of the Hebrew in this context, as well as in Isa. 43:1, "Do not fear, for I have redeemed you [= Israel]" and elsewhere in Isaiah 41–63. The action is not so much against sins of individuals as against material perils and hardships of Israel as a nation, but it is not unusual for it to be claimed by individuals.

Justice and Mercy

These words are frequently used in relation to Atonement as if they are characteristics of God that we should seek to understand, in order to endeavor to see their relevance, at least as metaphors of the processes of

Atonement. We usually think in terms of right and wrong determined by a set of laws. A just jury or judge, or equivalent, then decides whether a law has been broken, and reference is made to agreed penalties.

This idea of a penalty paid for sin originates in the Genesis story of the Fall. There the sin of Adam and Eve, disobedience to God's command not to eat the apple, was believed to be penalized by the physical death of every human thereafter. This belief was not difficult for the Jews in early times, and for many Jews at the time of Jesus and in the following years. For them, God took an extremely hard line on sin, and followed the human concept of justice coupled to penalties. The picture is of a God prepared and able to allow every human to die as the penalty for the "first sin." Today this view of God is unbelievable, since it omits any reference to the love of God, first realized by the prophets and fully expressed in the life of Jesus, the "divine human." It is also dangerous to assume that our human view of justice with penalties is God's view of justice combined with mercy. Furthermore, death is known to be a universal event in biological evolution. Disbelief in the literal reading of the sin that led to the Fall and its consequences, physical death, seems to rule out penalty theories of Atonement, and also makes difficult the tradition that it was the sacrificial death of Jesus that led to Atonement of human sin.

In terms of the human understanding of justice, only the guilty party can pay the penalty, which may well be punishment of some kind. The self-sacrifice of a substitute, although an act of love, is not an act of justice, but applying this understanding of justice should surely not be allowed to limit belief in the power of the love of God.

Forgiveness must come from the victims, since no one has authority to forgive sins committed against another. God can forgive only those sins that are against him, and even those are not to be forgiven if we do not forgive those who sin against us. This is evident in the Lord's Prayer (Matt. 6:12), and most clearly in Mark 11:25: "Whenever you stand praying, forgive, if you have anything against anyone; so that your Father in heaven may also forgive you your trespasses." The parable of the unforgiving servant in Matt. 18:21–35 makes the same point. We now recognize that the sins forgiven by the divine Son of man were sins against God. Reconciliation can take place only when the offer of for-giveness by the innocent party is fully accepted by the other party, and the adjustment of human relationships can take quite a long time, with inward anguish for suffering caused to another, and the realization that the guilt remains.

The NRSV version of the call of Isaiah, Isa. 6:6, reads, "Now that this [a live coal] has touched your lips, your guilt has departed and your sin is blotted out." The AV, the RV, the Revised English Bible and the Jerusalem Bible read "iniquity" instead of guilt. The differences between sin and iniquity are not immediately obvious. One commen-tator says, "[I]niquities are acts which a person's conscience recognizes as morally wrong and which may not offend God at all." And "sin is that which is displeasing to God, and may not affect the conscience." Guilt is a state or feeling of the person and is not an act. Forgiven persons know that the guilt attaches to them, even if others are prepared and able to forget it. The memory of the guilt may well help the sinner to avoid that sin in the future.

In the "satisfaction" teaching of Anselm, he used imagery from con-temporary society's treatment of actions that amounted to a "slight" upon the honor and dignity of a person, often a superior person or overlord. But humans were not good enough to make satisfaction to God for their sins, their "slight" upon the honor and dignity of God. They are already due to give total obedience as their duty to God, but satisfaction requires something extra, and that can be given only by God, as in the "God-man" of the Incarnation. Again this argument is no longer appropriate today since the social order on which this view of sin and this legal judgment is based no longer applies.

The justice of God is better understood as "righteousness," a con-cept that is more obviously appropriate to God than to humans. Right-eousness includes both the justice and the mercy of God, and attempts are made to determine when mercy can be granted and to what extent. In the Old Testament, mercy (Hebrew *chesed*) is how God keeps his covenant, and is sometimes translated "loving kindness." It is not related specifically to the forgiveness of sin, and this is in general true of the New Testament, with a notable exception in Luke 18:9–14, the parable in which the Pharisee and tax collector go to the temple to pray. The latter "standing far off, would not even look up to heaven, but was beating his breast and saying, 'God, be merciful to me, a sinner.'" Jesus comments, "I tell you, this man went down to his home justified rather than the other."

The question arises, "What happens after death?" God's relationship to each individual surely continues. Can anyone be fairly judged on the basis of his life and faith here? Human situations are so varied, from one leading to an easy acceptance of the Gospel to one where the absence of knowledge of the Gospel makes an explicit response impossible. Some very genuine and active seekers of truth find the evidence for what is to be believed most uncertain. The anguish of remorse felt by us cannot be escaped, nor can we avoid the need to continue spiritual growth, in the context of love. Our "righteousness" at death is a poor reflection of the righteousness of God.

Even the spiritual growth of such evil characters as Hitler and Stalin cannot be believed to be impossible in the light of the mercy and love of God. This is expressed in 2 Peter 3:9, "The Lord is . . . not wanting any to perish, but all to come to repentance." It is also made clear that God addressed the whole world in the act of Atonement, as in 2 Cor. 5:19, "in Christ God was reconciling the world to himself."

It may well be that the Roman Catholic belief in Purgatory, in which souls after death are purified from sins, or suffer punishment that remains to be endured, has a sound basis in reason. The belief is an example of a dynamic relationship between the Bible, tradition, and reason, and is held by the Roman and Eastern churches, with some differences concerning the nature of the punishment. Many of the Reformers rejected the doctrine, primarily because of the contemporary abuse of the buying of pardons, which were claimed to reduce the periods of suffering in Purgatory.

The Love of God

It was Peter Abelard (1079–1142) who first realized that the existing attempts to explain the Atonement in terms of substitutionary sacrifice made little or no reference to the love of God. The earliest

Old Testament picture of God made angry by sin, who responds to propitiatory sacrifices, was seriously challenged by the eighth-century prophet Hosea. In 6:6, the Lord says, "For I desire steadfast love and not sacrifice, the knowledge of God rather than burnt offerings." Hosea believed he was told by God to marry "a wife of whoredom" (1:2) and his experience of heartbreak, enraged rejection, and attempts at reconciliation led him to imagine how God felt about the unfaithfulness of Israel and Judah; yet God continued to love his people. Justice requires retribution, but love yearns to forgive, and Hosea heard God saying, "I will heal their disloyalty, I will love them freely, for my anger has turned from them" (14:4).

Abelard contributed to the establishment of theology as an academic discipline, a quest for truth, rather than a committed defense of the Christian faith. He saw the death of Jesus as almost exclusively a demonstration of the love of God inviting our response. "The purpose and cause of the Incarnation was that Christ might illuminate the world by his wisdom, and excite it to love of himself." The impact of the Cross is on human beings, not on God. Jesus sets a moral example, and we respond to his love instead of being governed by fear.

There is plenty of New Testament support for this approach. The story of the prodigal son shows the quality of the love of a human father: "while he was still far off, his father saw him and was filled with compassion; he ran and put his arms around him, and kissed him" (Luke 15:20). And the story shows the son's genuine remorse: "Father, I have sinned against heaven and before you; I am no longer worthy to be called your son" (Luke 15:21). The significance of love is most clearly stated in John 3:16, "For God so loved the world that he gave his only Son, so that everyone who believes in him may not perish but may have eternal life." In Rom. 5:8 we read, "God proves his love for us in that while we still were sinners Christ died for us." The theme is developed in 1 John 4:10, "in this is love, not that we loved God, but that he loved us, and sent his Son," but the writer cannot escape the added thought that the Son was "to be the atoning sacrifice [propitiation, RV] for our sins." The consequence is in the next verse, "Beloved, since God loved us so much, we also ought to love one another."

At the age of thirty-eight, Abelard, a lecturer in the cathedral school of Notre-Dame in Paris, fell in love with the seventeen-year-old Heloise, one of his pupils. A son was born, and they married, but the uncle of Heloise caused Abelard to be mutilated. He became a monk and Heloise took the veil. His great reputation as a teacher led to his becoming an abbot, but his views on the Trinity were condemned as heresy.

There is a link between Hosea's realization of the love of God and Abelard's recognition of its relevance to the understanding of Atonement. Both Hosea and Abelard, in very different ways, benefited from the depths of experience in human love.

Salvation

Salvation, as a term related to Atonement, is familiar in the religious sphere, and is also used for an escape from some military or political situations. In the religious sense *salvation* does not carry any preformed conception of sacrifice or ransom or justification, and *savior* can be used in place of *redeemer* without significant distortion of its meaning in context. It still invites the question, "What do you mean by salvation?" The religious answer will be largely in metaphorical usage of the terms already considered. Parallels are readily found in military and political circumstances, where again statements are needed to describe the intended meanings, both for *salvation* and *savior.*

In the Christian tradition as found in the Bible, salvation is from the wrath of God (Rom. 5:9) and the power of sin, whether in the meaning of an inner deficiency in humans or as the work of the Devil, or both. The treatment of sin as a universal peril came later to be replaced by sin as an individual peril, with individual paths to salvation. This enables the inclusion in salvation of the paths of other religions, including Judaism. Salvation then centers on God rather than on a single religion, almost like a Copernican revolution with God at the center and Christianity as one of the patterns of belief in orbit about, and permeated by, the Divine. This differs from the clear expression in, for example, Acts 4:12, "There is salvation in no one else, for there is no other name under heaven given among mortals by which we must be saved."

The act of salvation is seen not so much as a single act as part of the continuing pattern of creation, or as a "new creation" (2 Cor. 5:17), "so if anyone is in Christ, there is a new creation." Believers should "like newborn infants, long for the pure spiritual milk, so that by it [they] may grow into salvation" (1 Peter 2:2). Through the "good news" they "are being saved" (1 Cor. 15:1–2), and "the one who endures to the end will be saved" (Mark 13:13). These ideas bring out the need for people to continue good works so that they would be "justified by works and not by faith alone" (James 2:24) for "faith without works is also dead" (James 2:26).

The Need for Incarnation

Atonement is all about relationships; the relation of humankind to divinity, the relation of the Son, Jesus Christ, to the Father, the relation of each individual to God, and indeed to every member of humankind. Each knew the need for the other and suffered the lack of rapport that permeated the universe. It has been suggested that God, with his self-limited power to change the way the world is made, must have ached to fulfill his aim to create humans in his own image. As humans became more and more aware of their relation to God, it became increasingly desirable and indeed essential for there to be a mediator, a fusion of the divine and the human. God's response was to give his only beloved Son to the world, that through him the world might be saved and made aware of the love that abounds in the divine family, the Trinity of Father, Son, and Holy Spirit.

The mediator, Jesus Christ, had to experience what it is to be human, although he does not appear to have been ill, nor did he ever marry. In his conception, assistance was given by the power of the Holy Spirit, and then he started his mission. He needed to do this completely as a human, with no accessible divine might, so that he could cry in the depths of his suffering at the hands of humans, "My God, My God, why have you forsaken me?" (Mark 15:34). From his birth to Mary, through his childhood and adolescence, through his realization of his mission, and during his temptations to exploit his divine origin, he was in every sense human. His care for the sick and the wounded in spirit, his need to declare the new rules for spiritual survival as members and subjects of the Kingdom of God, and his despair at the lack of understanding even among his chosen disciples are all part of his inspired humanity. It was as a human that he showed his determination to complete the task he and God had set for him, right through to his condemnation to physical death. He accepted his suffering, compounded by the desertion of those he had loved and taught, and came to his final triumphal cry from the Cross, "It is finished [or accomplished]" (John 19:30). Throughout he was being human, experiencing what the Godhead, with all its powers of divine imagination, must have yet lacked.

After completing his life, governed by his self-limited ability to exercise the power of the divine, Jesus "refilled" his "emptied" self with ability to exercise those powers, exceeding the powers of created nature. This led to his Resurrection, to his granting of the powers of the Holy Spirit to the believers among humankind, and to his Ascension, and return to the divine family. The divine became one with the atoned in the New Creation, able to relate to all the human strengths and weaknesses, and able to offer to humans the fulfilment of the First Creation. What happened to Jesus did not change God's dealings with us. It changed God's relation to humanity. The burden of sin borne by each individual human could be taken away provided they saw their need, believed in the gospel of Jesus, repented of their shortcomings as God's creatures, forgave others their shortcomings, and were diligent in good works. Here, for humans, was the possibility of not only forgiveness but the riches of union or reunion with the Divine, an awareness of the omnipresence of God, the joys of eternal life, and reconciliation with both God and fellow humans.

Jesus is reported by John as saying, "The Father and I are one" (John 10:30), and he prayed: "Holy Father, protect them in your name that you have given me, so that they may be one, as we are one" (John 17:11). This was the realization of Atonement, so that Jesus could say, "I came not to judge the world, but to save the world" (John 12:47), and "take courage; I have conquered the world!" (John 16:33), and, in addressing the Father, "I glorified you on earth by finishing the work that you gave me to do" (John 17:4).

PREDESTINATION

The phrase "[those] that you have given me" (John 17:11), together with other passages, led some to believe in Predestination, the granting of salvation only to those who are selected by God. In Rom. 8:29 we read, "For those whom he foreknew he also predestined to be conformed to the image of his Son," and in verse 30, "And those whom he predestined he also called; and those whom he called he also justified; and those whom he justified he also glorified." According to Rom. 9:18, "he has mercy on whomsoever he chooses, and he hardens the heart of whomsoever he chooses." In Eph. 1:4 we read, "he chose us in Christ before the foundation of the world," and in verse 5, "He destined us for adoption as his children through Jesus Christ," and again in verse 11, "In Christ we have also obtained an inheritance, having been destined." First Peter 1:1–2 are addressed to "the exiles of the Dispersion . . . who have been chosen and destined by God." These passages seem to compromise the New Testament emphases on the universality of God's love and salvation, found for example in 1 Tim. 2:3–4 where Paul (or, more probably, a later author) declares that "God our Savior . . . desires everyone to be saved."

SUFFERING ON THE CROSS

There is no doubt that crucifixion entailed much physical suffering, made worse by the sort of treatment that Jesus suffered before the actual crucifixion. Many men underwent similar extremes of suffering, but for Jesus there was the added experience of mental and spiritual suffering associated with his sense of mission, and the failure of his disciples to listen and understand what was his mission. Yet Jesus accepted that "the Son of Man must undergo great suffering . . . and be killed" (Mark 8:31). He submitted to the will of God asking the Father to "remove this cup from me, yet not what I want, but what you want" (Mark 14:36).

The recorded sayings from the cross are frequently used in sermons and in hymns to emphasize how terrible were the sufferings. It is often suggested that it is in part our sins that caused that suffering, and as a timeless metaphor this can be accepted. Another suggestion is that our day-to-day sins increase the continuing suffering of Jesus on the cross. These are good examples of the spiritual and heartfelt imagination of the cost, and continuing cost, of the Atonement. It is the evidence of personal devotional conviction that supports them. The images of Atonement, and attempts to explain Atonement, are deeply and extensively spelled out in hymns and devotional writings. To take them literally sometimes sets up a serious barrier to the absorption of divine truths that are beyond literal statements. Much as it might be arguable that such images and explanations should be minimized or abandoned, the spiritual and emotional damage that this would produce will persuade the large majority of believers that it would be seriously inadvisable to make large or sudden changes.

The theological principle *"lex orandi: lex credendi"* comes to mind, sometimes translated as "the official prayers of the Church reveal the official beliefs of the Church." When the instinctive prayers of worshipers begin to adapt to the acceptable images and explanations of the Atonement, and the official prayers begin to respond to the inevitable pressures from the body of believers, then there might be explicit corresponding adjustments in official statements of belief. Examples of this can already be found in relation to the role of women in the Church.

An Outline of Atonement

Having given special attention to the evidence, both for the event and for the various interpretations, it is now possible to see an outline within which the richness of spiritual interpretations can find their place.

In chapter 10, "Today's Creation Story: January 1, 2000," it was noted that

> God saw that it was good, but it was not good enough, for free
> will led to sin and suffering, and guilt and disbelief could lead
> to despair and the death of the human spirit. So God sent his

only Son, the Word made flesh, who dwelt among us, as Jesus of Nazareth, suffered, died and was raised from the dead, and showed his glory, full of grace and truth. And that was the beginning of the New Creation.

Atonement was firmly established and practiced through sacrifices in the Jewish community, and the ideas were therefore well known to Jewish converts to Christianity. Gentile Christians came to share this understanding and brought to it Greek ideas that are most clearly expressed in John's Gospel.

Early Christians abandoned the Jewish sacrifices of the Day of Atonement, but found that the idea of sacrifice had some vital relation to the death of Jesus and its purpose. They also found the concepts of redemption and ransom to be relevant, and the concepts of justice and mercy were explored. None of these approaches is fully convincing or attractive to many present-day Christian believers, nor to genuine seekers. Nevertheless, the metaphorical values of these images and reasoning continue to be used and cherished by those same believers.

The more spiritual and even mystical approaches primarily presented in John's Gospel may be found closer to the perceptions of many of today's inquirers and believers. The essential elements are the love of God in the Incarnation of the Son of God, his total humanity including his death, and his Resurrection and Ascension. Thereby was made possible the Atonement (at-one-ment) with the complete unity of humanity with divinity. Individuals could enter into this relationship by repentance and belief in Jesus, coincident with forgiving the sins of others, and a determined attempt to practice good works, leading to an enhanced realization of the presence of God in their lives, and the love of God for the whole world.

The evidence for the belief in Atonement is found in the positive experiences of large numbers of Christians throughout the ages, and by the present-day experiences of relationships between humans, and experiences relating individuals to God. It is the evidence of reasoning based on historical records, primarily the New Testament, and on individual experience within various traditions.

The most persuasive thoughts about Atonement are seen in the love of the Father in the Incarnation of the Son, in the taking up of humanity into the Trinity, in the gift of the Holy Spirit, in the spiritual significance of the associated human experiences, and in the indelible awareness of mystery largely outside the verifiable evidence of human experience.

CHAPTER 17

The Evolution of Belief?

OR MANY PEOPLE, it is a matter of the deepest personal conviction that God chose to create the universe by evolution. First there was cosmological evolution, producing galaxies, stars, and planets. Our earth was formed 4,500 million years ago and its composition and geological formations evolved until life was possible, about 3,850 million years ago. Biological evolution produced the oldest multicellular fossils about 1,800 million years ago. Fossils give evidence of communities of simple multicellular animals some 600 million years ago. The branch on the "tree of life" bearing ancestors of humans diverged from the chimpanzee branch some 6 to 8 million years ago. Humanity has been identified as a distinct species from *Homo sapiens* fossils of 200,000 to 150,000 years ago.

CHARACTERISTICS OF EVOLUTION

In most evolutionary processes there is a growth in time of the number of types of the subject studied, which can be placed in an ordered sequence with identifiable links, possibly starting with a known ancestor, revealed by careful categorization of physical form, degrees of complexity, or qualities of activity. For the physical universe this is a well-known feature. The processes in plants and animals are now explicitly revealed by studies of the molecule controlling life forms, DNA. Side by side with the recognition of the facts of evolution there are usually theories that attempt to explain the phenomenon. When there are competing processes it is common to look for evidence of survival of the fittest, usually illustrated by transitional forms. It is also common to discover vestigial features in the latest organisms, which have no continuing role to play.

The enhanced success of procreation by species exhibiting two different and complementary sexes can be explained in terms of the introduction of a new "sexual selection" process. This operates in parallel with the "natural selection" driven by survival of the fittest. Males will select partners using one set of instinctive criteria, reinforced by conscious criteria, and females will select partners by a different set of instinctive criteria, also reinforced by conscious criteria. These criteria may well include potential for survival and spread of the family. Darwin suggested that the need to develop features that attracted the opposite sex was one of the most important factors in the increase in size of the human brain. These features would have included characteristically human capacities for language, music, morality and altruism, and possibly wit and humor. The introduction of human selection, which includes conscious selection of criteria, can be seen as allowing the development of human faculties along lines that may appear to be "evolutionary." However, so many events spring from the exercise of free will, that influence intellectual activities, that it would be dangerous to believe that all intellectual achievements are properly described as the direct products of natural evolution.

There is a misleading tendency to think of evolution as occurring in a straight line by a continuous process. It needs to be emphasized that numerous strands are involved in evolution, with branching and parallel sequences, some of which die out. There is also continual evolution, rather than a continuous progression, with almost discontinuous jumps forward, and at times there seem to be steps backwards to an earlier stage, sometimes caused by catastrophic mass extinctions, sometimes with renewed evolution along dissimilar paths.

EVOLUTION OF MENTAL PROCESSES?

It is evident from fossils that the brain size of humans and their closest ancestors has increased in the last three million years. It is therefore reasonable to look for evolution or the development of the brain and mental processes, as recognized by Darwin in relation to the role of two sexes discussed above. These developments are revealed in a variety of ways, in self-awareness, community awareness and complexity, moral attitudes, language and logical and mathematical reasoning, the development of tools, and many art forms such as painting, sculpture, and music, and the first elements of religious belief. The characteristics of societies and cultures have developed in a variety of forms and types. Mathematics came to flourish and the physical and other sciences made significant advances, leading to developments in technology. These had, and still have, an impact on our patterns and standards of living, including the means of waging wars that contribute to survival of the fittest. In particular there have been great advances in the transmission and storage of information in both literal and visual forms, combined with the power of computers, supplementing the capacities and powers of our brains. Insofar as these developments depended largely on the conscious decisions of humans, with little obvious influence from natural processes, it is not solely a matter of "evolution" based on random processes.

DEVELOPMENT OF RELIGIOUS BELIEF

Being convinced that there has been, and still is, an increase of mental qualities and activities, it is perhaps reasonable to look for the parallel development of spiritual qualities and activities, leading to richer kinds of religious belief. Care should be taken not to divide a human into body, mind, and spirit (or soul), as if they were separate entities, when the more convincing understanding is of one person with material, mental and spiritual functions that characterize an individual.

A question that frequently arises is, "How does God create by evolution?" An extreme atheist answer is, "There is no need for God, science can explain everything." Of course, that is in itself a belief, not able to be proved or disproved, and it is also a belief that develops with the progress of science. The activity of God in creation by evolution is linked to the nature of the providence of God in the present-day universe. There is no simple answer based on generally available evidence to the simple question, "Does God interact with nature?" There is, however, plenty of evidence of religious believers who are convinced that God and humans live in an ongoing relationship, characterized by loving forgiveness. This relationship between humans and God thrives on spiritual thoughts, flashes of imagination, and awareness of mystery embedded in awe, and it is nourished in worship. For those among such believers who are convinced of the natural processes of evolution, it is not difficult to believe that God, in some sense, is controlling the seminal stages in an overarching manner consistent with the truths of science, some of which have yet to be discovered. It is in principle difficult, if not impossible, to adduce evidence for either the presence or absence of divine intervention, other than that claimed by such individuals or groups of individuals.

Some religious believers are so convinced of the constraints of science that they cannot accept that the God in whom they believe interacts with nature. This position makes sense only if it is linked to the belief that enough is known of science to underpin this extreme religious belief. It should, however, be admitted that the evidence for believing in the interactions of God with nature is, strictly speaking, not itself repeatable scientific evidence, however personally convincing.

The beliefs that are predominant in our thoughts and relationships, and relevant for the investigation of the development of religious belief, include the image of God, the nature of men and women, the role of the Devil, God's actions in Incarnation and Atonement, and life after death. Some would combine these elements in the subject of the nature of the Church, and others would add many other important aspects of belief such as the role of the Bible, and the development of creeds.

The processes involved in development of religious belief cover personal experience, family interactions, involvement in wider society, and, most important, the activities within the Church or religious groups, relating in particular to the Bible and creeds. I shall not engage in a history of the Jewish faith and the Christian churches. Instead I shall select a few of the more tractable and important changes of belief over the millennia. Beliefs related to the Creation have changed considerably, and have already been addressed. The creation stories before Genesis had two features that are largely abandoned in Genesis, namely a multiplicity of gods and consequential conflicts between divinities. That there is evidence in the Old Testament of vestigial beliefs from this earlier period is in itself evidence of development of belief. As already considered, beliefs about creation have been definitively influenced by the progress in science since the mid-nineteenth century. Belief in biological evolution casts doubt on the clear belief in Genesis that humans were specially created, morally perfect, and simultaneously given a soul. It is not possible to believe that the first sin, as identified in Genesis, was the cause of universal physical death, since the natural sequence in evolution is birth, survival, procreation, and physical death, occurring among animals a long time before humans had evolved. One of the unanswered theological questions is "Why did God create animals that have often had to suffer in an attempt to survive?"

MEN AND WOMEN

Beliefs about men and women have, for thousands of years, been dominated by the beliefs of men. From time to time, remarkable women have stood out, for example, in the Old Testament the prophetess and judge Deborah, and Jael, who killed Sisera with a tent peg (Judg. 4:4–10, 17–21).

In the New Testament it is clear that Jesus related to women much more sympathetically than was conventional. He spoke to the Samaritan woman at the well, to her surprise, and his disciples were astonished (John 4:7–30). Jesus accepted graciously the washing and anointing of his feet by a woman "who was a sinner" (Luke 7:37–50). Jesus rescued from stoning the woman caught in adultery (John 8:3–11).

The role of women in the discovery of the empty tomb, as evidence of the Resurrection, has already been noted, but strangely they are not mentioned by Paul. He emphasizes in 1 Cor. 11:2–16 that the man is the head of his wife, arguing that women were created for the sake of men, as also in 1 Tim. 2:11–13 where he adds, "I permit not a woman to teach." Again in 1 Cor. 14:33–36 he declares that "women should be silent in the churches" and "should be subordinate." There is a suggestion that verses 34–35 are later additions as verse 36 is a natural continuation of verse 33, and some ancient authorities put verses 34–35 after verse 40. If verses 34–35 are omitted, this would agree with Rom. 16:1–15 in which he sends greetings to no fewer than twenty-six named individuals of whom ten are women, who worked with him. They include Junia (v. 7) who, paired with Andronicus, as usual for man and wife, were "prominent among the apostles." (Some doubt this reading and prefer the masculine amendment, Junias, which may be a "scandalous mistranslation," since no other occurrence of Junias is known, whereas the feminine Junia is very well attested.)

Throughout the history of the Church there have been women saints and powerful abbesses and prioresses. Today the part played by women in church services and administration is increasingly obvious and appreciated. Some of those who use the Bible as their definitive guide in such matters still influence attitudes to women in the Church, but significant changes in the rest of society have obliged a rethink.

Important recent developments include the first ordination of women to the priesthood in the Church of England, in 1994, and in other Anglican churches over many years in many countries. There are women bishops in Anglican churches in America, Canada, and New Zealand. The Scottish Episcopal Church voted in 2003 to allow the appointment of women bishops, and they could soon be in place. The Church of England has set up a theological commission to examine the question of women bishops. The possibility of women priests in the Roman Catholic Church is openly discussed, together with the advantages of revision of the celibacy of the clergy. Devotion to Mary, the mother of Jesus, has received little emphasis in Protestant churches. Some Roman Catholics are uneasy about excessive devotion to Mary and the theology that lies behind it. There is increasing awareness of the contributions that women can make to the development of theology. In United Kingdom universities and colleges approximately one half of the students of theology are women, and there are increasing numbers of women professors of theology. There is evidence here of important developments not only of religious belief but also of the nature of society.

ANGELS, FALLEN ANGELS, DEMONS, AND THE DEVIL

A problem similar to that of the nature of God arises with respect to belief in angels, fallen angels, demons, and their leader, the Devil or Satan. Archaeological discoveries have told us much about the development of religion in countries adjacent to Palestine. In 1928 a Syrian farmer accidentally discovered ancient tombs near Ras Shamra, in western Syria, containing numerous cuneiform tablets with political and religious texts of the ancient kingdom of Ugarit. They date from the fifteenth to the thirteenth centuries B.C.E. and refer to many of the gods known from the Bible as Canaanite deities. It is clear that early Israelite religion was not so discontinuous from Canaanite religion as was once thought. There are Ugaritic stories of fallen astral deities, that is, angels, notably Ashtar (or Astarte, 1 Kings 11:5, worshiped by Solomon) who attacked the throne of Baal, the storm deity.

Jesus is reported as saying in Luke 10:18, "I watched Satan fall from heaven like a flash of lightning." This parallels the poetry of Isa. 14:12, referring to the fall of Babylon, "How you are fallen from heaven, O Day Star, son of Dawn," and lyrical passages with vivid imagery in Rev. 12:7–9 relating to war in heaven when "The great dragon was thrown down [to the earth], that ancient serpent, who is called the Devil and Satan."

In Gen. 3:1 we read, "[T]he serpent was more crafty than any other wild animal that the Lord God had made." He is not therefore believed to be self-existent, having been created by God, and therefore in this reading there is no question of the dualism and conflict found in earlier creation stories, and developed in Greek and Middle East Gnosticism. He tempts Eve, and is identified as the Devil in Wisd. 2:24, "through the devil's envy death entered the world." In Gen. 6:2, "sons of God" refers to divine members of God's heavenly assembly, that is, to angels. This parallels other Ugaritic, Phoenician, and Ammonite references. In Genesis male angels took wives for themselves of the fair daughters of humans, producing the Nephilim (6:4), "heroes that were of old, warriors of renown." The action and subsequent wickedness of humankind led to the story of the Flood. The dating of these texts is uncertain and care is needed in seeking to find evidence for the development of the belief in "fallen angels" toward the idea of a single leader, the Devil or Satan. The same is true for Zechariah 3–6, where God talks with both Satan and Joshua. The influences of seventh-century B.C.E. Zoroastrianism, and of Persian dualism, are not clear. However, by the end of the third century B.C.E. there is belief in the archenemy of God and humankind.

Satan in the New Testament has a variety of names, for example, Devil (Matt. 4:5), Tempter (Matt. 4:3), Satan (Matt. 4:10), Beelzebul (Matt. 10:25), Adversary (1 Peter 5:8), the Evil One (1 John 5:18), Apollyon or Abaddon (Rev. 9:11), the Ancient Serpent (Rev. 12:9), and the Accuser of our Comrades (Rev. 12:10). Satan and his demons are commonly believed to incite humans to evil deeds, and cause illness, and as such were part of contemporary beliefs, including those of Jesus.

During the medieval period, the belief in a personalized Devil, often referred to as Lucifer, was supported by many paintings, usually showing him in red, with horns and a forked tail. Today, belief in the Devil, and in angels, is widespread in Christianity, but some Christians are more cautious. The same is true for belief in archangels, referred to only twice in the New Testament (1 Thess. 4:16 in the second coming of the Lord, and in Jude 9 where the Archangel Michael "contended with the devil"). The development of medieval demonology identified nine orders of angels: (1) seraphim; (2) cherubim; (3) thrones; (4) dominions; (5) virtues; (6) powers; (7) principalities; (8) archangels; and (9) angels. In Col. 1:16 the creation of 3, 4, 6, and 7 is mentioned. In Rom. 8:38 there is mention of 6, 7 and 9. Cherubim are given a fantastic description in Ezek 1:4–28 and seraphim in Isa. 6:2–6. The attempt to find evidence for these beliefs, other than mentions in the Bible, particularly by Jesus, founders on diverse invincible personal convictions.

INCARNATION AND ATONEMENT

These subjects have been considered in chapter 16, but it is relevant here to comment on evidence for the development of these beliefs. In the earliest records from various countries, it is frequently stated that priests and kings were incarnate divinities. The body of Zoroaster (630–550 B.C.E.) was believed to have fallen from heaven as rain that was taken in by heifers and fed as milk to his mother. In Jainism, Jina (599–527 B.C.E.) was believed to have descended from heaven, and grew up sinless and omniscient. Hindu avatars were incarnations, especially of Vishnu, and could appear in many places at the same time. Avatars were believed not to be afflicted by the full range of human suffering, and retained part of their divine knowledge and power. Mahayana Buddhism developed in India in the third century B.C.E. and presents Buddha as coming to earth as a teacher in response to human sufferings. The expansion of the Roman empire, between 250 B.C.E. and 150 C.E., led to the assimilation of elements of the conquered cultures, in particular from the Greek civilization developed between 600 and 200 B.C.E. In Roman and Greek mythology it was believed that gods sometimes assumed human forms and married humans.

It is not easy to find a path of progress through these various beliefs about Incarnation. Christian beliefs as represented in Paul's writings point to the existence of Christ before the creation (for example, I Cor. 8:6, "Christ, through whom are all things and through whom we exist"). Later writings confirm this idea, Col. 1:16, "all things have been created through him and for him," and Heb. 1:1–2, "[God] . . . has spoken to us by a Son, whom he appointed heir of all things, through whom he also created the worlds." The best-known expression is in John 1:1–5, "He [the Word] was in the beginning with God. All things came into being through him." This is close to making Jesus the Father's agent in creation. Later Christian theology, especially within the Eastern tradition, held that the aim of the Incarnation was the transformation of human nature into one compatible with the divine. The Incarnation beliefs led to the development of the doctrine of the Trinity, with Christ fully divine and fully human, and one with the Holy Spirit.

Atonement, the reconciliation of sinful humans with God, was well established in the Jewish faith in the time of Jesus. Two distinct approaches are evident in the Old Testament, the older one associated with ritual sacrifices, from the earliest recorded times, and the later one with the prophets. The Day of Atonement for hundreds of years was marked by special sacrifices. These were discontinued during the Babylonian Exiles (597, 586–538 B.C.E.), reestablished on the return from Exile, and finally abandoned after the destruction of the Temple in 70 C.E. The eighth-century prophets rejected sacrifices with their superstitions and unworthy ideas of God, as in Hosea 6:6, "For I desire steadfast love and not sacrifice, the knowledge of God rather than burnt-offerings," and in Micah 6:6–8, "Shall I come before him with burnt offerings, with calves a year old? . . . He has told you, O mortal, what is good; and what does the Lord require of you but to do justice, and to love kindness, and to walk humbly with your God?" See also Deut. 10:12–13 (seventh-fifth century B.C.E.).

The ideas of sacrifice were therefore easily related by the first Christians to the crucifixion of Jesus, but needed to be rethought when large numbers of Gentiles were attracted to the Church. This followed the struggle between unnamed Judeans, who wanted to preserve within Christianity certain Jewish features, such as circumcision and special food, and Paul, who saw that Gentiles were equally inspired by the gospel message and should be treated equally. The question was resolved when Peter and James agreed with Paul at the Apostolic Council in Jerusalem about 50 C.E. (Acts 15:4–29, see also Romans 9–11).

The principal New Testament ideas relating to Atonement, other than sacrifice, centered on redemption and ransom. The society of the time was familiar with the redemption of slaves by a ransom paid to the owners, and the terminology and pictures used were easily adopted. Later the images used were developed by assuming that the death of Jesus was the ransom paid to the Devil, or that his resurrection was victory over the Devil. The key to the understanding of Atonement, whatever the images and theories adduced, was clearly anchored in the person of Jesus, and in his death and resurrection. Atonement was an intense reality for early Christians, and still is so today, as expressed in the simple statement, "Christ died for our sins," and it is seen as a supreme act of grace and the free love of God. An essential element in all the accepted doctrines was the belief that Jesus was both fully divine and fully human, although it was also believed that in some sense Jesus "emptied himself" of his divinity (Phil. 2:5–11).

Theologians developed theories or doctrines of the Atonement that found their place in relation to the changing practices and beliefs in local societies. The Western and Roman church emphasized the role of justice, conceived in contemporary and local terms and images, such as penalty, acquittal, justification, sacrifice, and expiation. Propitiation was seen as a penance due to the slight upon the dignity of God, as would be required for local contemporary dignitaries. It was believed that Jesus paid the penalty for human sin by suffering on the cross, God having "made him to be sin" (2 Cor. 5:21), and having felt that he had been deserted by God. The doctrines in terms of "a just punishment" or "giving an adequate satisfaction" or the traditional "offering of a sufficient sacrifice" largely exclude the idea of divine loving forgiveness so evident in contemporary Jewish understanding and made explicit in the sayings of Jesus. Abelard, about 1100 C.E., was the first to give emphasis to the role of the love of God in Atonement. The love of God the Father is perhaps nowhere so clear as in the parable of the prodigal son (Luke 15:18–24).

The Eastern and Orthodox church, with its Hellenistic philosophical background, was more concerned with salvation as an entry into a right relationship with God, brought about by the resurrected Christ and the continuing grace of the Holy Spirit, following an initiating act of Atonement. "All of us ... are being transformed into the same image from one degree of glory to another; for this comes from the Lord, the Spirit" (2 Cor. 3:18). And "you . . . may become participants in the divine nature" (2 Peter 1:4). The process was frequently called "deification" (*theosis* in Greek), restoring "the image of God" in which humankind was believed to have been made perfect.

Neither belief, in Incarnation and Atonement, can be described as the result of evolution in the sense of a process within nature. The beliefs certainly developed, primarily as a result of the experiences and thoughts of humans.

LIFE AFTER DEATH

Archaeological evidence from burials of the dead, more than 40,000 years ago, suggests that belief in some kind of life after death originated in the earliest times of humanity. The provision of food and drink implies a belief in a spirit dwelling within the dead, and is found in some ancient Egyptian and Canaanite burials. When the concept of right and wrong developed, and the role of the divine in the history of humankind became a subject of increasing speculation and conviction, it became natural to believe in different states of survival according to the moral status of the individual. In some cultures, as in India, the spirit was conceived as entering into another body at death, and belief in restoration or reanimation provided preservation of personal identity. The idea of reincarnation as a higher or lower character led some to believe in a never-ending series of births and deaths, from which there could be an escape in Nirvana by eliminating lust, hatred, greed, and ignorance. Higher reincarnations could be into a superior person, and lower ones into an animal or the spirit of a tree, beliefs found in Hinduism, Buddhism, and Jainism, and also among Greeks, such as Pythagoras and Plato.

Beliefs in the fate of dead individuals had parallels in the fate of nations. In early Israel the "Day of Yahweh" was a coming day of battle, at first thought of as a great victory, but some prophets feared complete destruction. It was in this context that the idea of a military Messiah was developed, possibly a "King of the Jews" to break the Roman yoke, and increasing unrest led to the rebellion of 66–70 C.E. and the final destruction of the Temple. Jesus was careful to disassociate himself from temporal kingship, and spoke rather of the Kingdom of Heaven, but the accusation "King of the Jews" led to his death.

After the Resurrection of Jesus, belief was consolidated in the Second Coming of Christ and in the coming of the Kingdom, based on a number of sayings, such as "Truly I tell you, this generation will not pass away until all these things have taken place" (Mark 13:30). "These things" include "the Son of Man coming in clouds with great power and glory" (13:26). The nearness in time, as in 1 Peter 4:7, "The end of all things is near," is qualified by the inability to predict the date. Jesus says "about that day or hour no one knows, neither the angels in heaven, nor the Son, but only the Father" (Mark 13:32). This has not prevented Christian individuals and groups from predicting specific dates that come and go without deterring the relatively few believers in the dates. A similar belief is found in Islam, with the expectation of the reincarnation of a great prophet from the past. The Muslim messiah Mahdi is expected to reveal the truth more fully, and to produce better social conditions on earth.

The difficulty in identifying a related sequence of events and beliefs arises from the lack of evidence of connections between the several strands of belief in the after life. Causal links producing the changes of belief are also unconvincing, with spontaneous developments seeming to be more common.

HEAVEN AND HELL

Evidence of belief in heaven and hell is found in many religions. Evidence supporting the belief rests almost entirely on a combination of (1) a sense of right and wrong, (2) a recognition of the place of divine judgment, and (3) a belief that life after death will involve reward in heaven or punishment in hell.

One meaning of "heaven" (*ouranos* in Greek) is simply the sky, as in Mark 13:31, "Heaven and earth will pass away." It is also the abode of "angels of heaven" (Matt. 24:36, etc.), and "is the throne of God" (Matt. 5:34). Jesus, in John 6:38, says, "I have come down from heaven," and this is echoed in the Creed together with "ascended into heaven." At the baptism of Jesus there was "a voice from heaven" (Matt. 3:17).

The phrase "kingdom of Heaven" is used twenty-nine times in Matthew (AV), and in Matthew only, being preferred to "kingdom of God" (in AV, five times in Matthew, thirteen in Mark, twenty in Luke, and two in John) but with a similar meaning, namely the kingship of God rather than his dwelling place. This is spelled out in six separate parables in Matthew 13; indeed in Matt. 13:34 it is reported that "Jesus told the crowds all these things in parables; and without a parable he told them nothing."

Paradise is promised by the crucified Jesus to the repentant crucified robber, "Truly I tell you, today you will be with me in Paradise" (Luke 23:43). Paradise was originally a Persian word for a nobleman's park or garden. The rabbis thought there was one paradise in heaven and one in hell. It appears to be a pleasant place for the righteous dead. Paul tells how he was "caught up to the third Heaven" (2 Cor. 12:2) later expressed as "up into Paradise" (2 Cor. 12:4).

Hell is the English translation of *Sheol* in Hebrew, and *Hades* in Greek, the abode of departed spirits. An alternative translation of Sheol is "the Pit" (Ps. 28:1, Isa. 14:15), which finds a parallel in Rev. 9:1ff. as "the bottomless pit," with its fire and brimstone (burning sulphur) and tor-ture. In Luke 16:23, in contrast to the poor man, the rich man Lazarus goes to Hades, "where he was being tormented." In Mark 9:47–49, Jesus is reported as saying, "And if your eye causes you to stumble, tear it out; it is better for you to enter the kingdom of God with one eye than to have two eyes and to be thrown into hell, where their worm never dies, and the fire is never quenched. For everyone will be salted with fire." These beliefs are vividly portrayed in paintings such as those of Hieronymus Bosch.

After books of the Bible had been formally defined in "The Canon of Scripture," a number of other books were considered worthy of respect for their records of developing beliefs and practices. In one of these, 1 Enoch 22:1, dated about 170 B.C.E., four hollows are described in a large mountain of hard rock. They are for the reception of the spir-its of the souls of the dead. The first hollow with a bright spring of water is for the spirits of the righteous. The second is for the spirits of the sinners who have not yet been punished. The third is for martyrs. The fourth is for sinners who had endured suffering in their lives. These ideas arose from beliefs in the resurrection of the dead for judgment, and served to show that the dead were not left in one undifferentiated state between death and final judgment. There may be a link here to "Purgatory."

Many Christians hold on to the promise of heaven and the fear of hell in a vague or ambiguous way. Some churches teach explicit detailed beliefs in heaven and paradise, and in hell and punishment, but others are more restrained.

IS EVOLUTION THE RIGHT WORD IN RELATION TO RELIGIOUS BELIEF?

It was noted that the key features in evolving systems are large numbers of events or beliefs related in some way, each to another, able to be put in a sequence revealing many small changes and perhaps a few larger ones. Evidence of a process leading to change, and competition or an equivalent reason for survival of changes, would be a natural parallel to the convincing pattern of biological evolution.

Such clear-cut circumstances are rarely found in relation to the development of religious beliefs. Historical events and free human choice feature significantly, especially the blending of cultures arising from military conquest. Changes in social patterns, associated with altered wealth in communities, often lead to changes in details of belief, or criteria for choice. Relative wealth with increased leisure provides occasions for advances in education, leading to speculations concerning such great themes as the nature of God, creation of the universe, the purpose of life, and conditions in the afterlife. These developments became significant in the times of the ancient Greeks, after about 500 B.C.E., and led to the expansion of interest in astronomy (and astrology), mathematics, and the beginnings of physical and other sciences. The impact on beliefs then became apparent, but nearly always with strong opposition from the majority of believers in the existing patterns.

This clinging to the old in the presence of new ideas is a characteristic of nearly all religious communities, from ancient times right up to today. In many religions this follows the identification and correlation of generally accepted written records, notably the Old Testament and later the New Testament to form the Bible. For Muslims there is the Qur'an, and similarly more ancient writings for Eastern religions. In turn these official writings become supported by official creeds or

"Confessions," and these make it all the more difficult for individuals and groups of believers to evaluate changes in related beliefs, whether they be scientific, political, sociological, or ethical. Within Christianity the most remarkable refusal to review religious beliefs relates to the structure of the solar system, unchallenged for nearly 1,600 years. The mid-nineteenth-century evidence for biological evolution, collected by Darwin, was reinforced by the evidence, from the 1950s onwards, of the role of DNA signatures. A number of sizable groups still try to take literally almost every word of the Bible, in particular the creation story and the Fall, in the first few chapters of Genesis.

In circumstances like these it is not possible to interpret changes of belief as part of an evolutionary process. The reason is clear. Evolution is thought of most persuasively in relation to physical and geological evolution, and the natural selection in biological evolution. In these, humankind plays no part except in the very latest stages of biological evolution, in particular as the result of evolution of sexual reproduction, as noted above. Once humans came into existence their ability to influence the processes of nature took effect. This is evident in the human selection of animals and plants for "selective breeding," with remarkable results, from the large varieties of dogs to the wide range of colors and forms of flowers. Now that genetic research has made such astonishing advances, there is technical know-how for so-called genetic engineering, selecting desirable human characteristics. Even the environment is subject to the effects of technological developments in human activity, for example, through genetically modified crops. There seems to be no overall natural selection process to fashion our religious beliefs, except to the extent of those beliefs that are either the result of sexual awareness or the product of reason, with the added assumption that sexual awareness and reason or logic depend on the degree to which the brain has evolved, in capacity, complexity, and character. In the development of science, the direction of progress is decided by human reason or choice, and likewise the rate of progress, but there seem to be inexorable advances with survival of the fittest scientific theories, and abandoning of those considered inadequate.

Each individual is free to choose what he believes, even if there are some limits set by the power of authority in certain groups, such as a church or a society. This is true for all religions, not just for Christianity. It would be interesting in this respect to view Christianity in the context of other world religions. This is, however, outside the aims of this book.

CHAPTER 18

Evidence from Meditation and Prayer

MEDITATION

MEDITATION is a reasoning activity of the brain, often in the form of words and phrases, but also in formless ideas, directional emotions, and even mathematical and visual representation. I once heard it identified, to remove the fears that some have about meditation, as what men do when they are shaving. Every mathematician in trying to solve problems undertakes a kind of meditation. Many scientists report that a problem explored last thing at night sometimes leads, on waking, to a new avenue of thought or even a solution. Is this perhaps meditation during sleep?

In this attempt to characterize meditation, I have not yet mentioned God. Religious meditation is a conscious encounter with God with a wide range of methods, common to most religions. Christian meditation uses a well-known vocabulary of words, with phrases, images, and tactile aids (such as a rosary), music, and even aromas and special effects of lighting. There are many and varied claims of the value of religious meditation that concentrates on the nature of God, and his activities in his creation. Such meditation has been known to influence a person's beliefs, and to that extent it is the source of evidence leading to "evidence-based belief." Most Christian meditation produces an enhanced awareness of God's presence and tends to confirm the beliefs on which the meditation is based. It also reinforces awareness of trust in God, which, together with realized beliefs, forms the very basis of the Christian faith, and stimulates the desire to love one's neighbor.

Some people find it helpful to make written notes during meditation, not in an attempt to produce a coherent report on the session, but in order to stimulate new thoughts and relate them to previous notes. Writing during meditation can often concentrate the attention most effectively. If the meditation does relate to preparing a talk, or writing a book (!), then being able to return to a position reached the previous day, or earlier, brings out any changes of thought or opportunities for revision, or points of attachment for developing ideas. Sometimes it is possible to plan a series of meditations under subheadings, provided these headings do not become so constraining that the liberating features of productive meditation are inhibited.

Meditation is possible not only for individuals but also for groups. It can be conducted in silence, but is sometimes able to accommodate interruptions of a helpful kind. By listening to the thoughts of others it is inevitable that some of their ideas are different from one's own. This new evidence then awaits a considered evaluation; it is a kind of evidence that can be useful for confirming or modifying one's beliefs.

PRAYER

Prayer is a conscious interchange of thoughts with God, a joint experience of the human with the divine. It is most usually, on the human side, in the form of words, in phrases or sentences, but not infrequently prayer takes the form of speechless awareness, a spiritual and religious experience, a comforting or disturbing realization of the presence of God and of his providential activities, and a moral urge to love our neighbors, near and far. Attempts to put our prayer into words may enhance our ability to express ourselves, yet at the same time it will impress on us the ineffable qualities of the experience. Whatever the occasion, private, in family or group, or in public worship, it is a uniquely personal experience.

Although we may not be inclined explicitly to relate our prayer to our beliefs, the underlying motivation for prayer comes from beliefs and habits acquired throughout our lives. We might wonder therefore how belief-based prayer becomes evidence for belief. Perhaps it would be better to consider prayer as producing evidence of confirmation of beliefs, or evidence for revision of some aspects of belief. Trust in God is itself an explicit form of belief, peculiarly strengthening but able to be the source of distressing doubt, as for example in the face of unrelieved suffering brought before God in prayer.

There is much evidence of the influence of prayer not only on the individual who is praying but also on others. The others may or may not know that somebody is praying for them, and may never associate events in their lives with the prayerful actions of others. At this stage, it would be easy to retell some of the many stories of answered prayer, by which it is usually inferred that specific requests led to positive answers. I shall not present such evidence of answered prayer because it is so frequently questioned, with attempts to explain away coincidences. I recognize, however, how powerful is the experience of answered prayer for the individual concerned, whether as the petitioner or as the recipient of the results of the intercessions of others. For a sick person to know that others are praying for him or her often leads to a recognition of a veritable raft of prayer, supporting the sick person's positive thoughts and reinforcing that person's awareness of the presence, the concern, and the action of God. When this happens to an individual it becomes very powerful evidence of the value of belief in the existence and nature of God. We must be prepared to accept that there may be very good divine reasons why the answer to some petitionary or intercessory prayer appears to be "No." One reason, considered in chapter 15 on suffering, could be that God as a result of Kenotic Creation cannot do certain things. If the reasons can, in retrospect, be recognized and accepted as persuasive, that too can be evidence of the action of God, and be the basis for developing belief. It all depends on existing trust in God, and on its continuation as a trust impressed upon the person at prayer as a necessary consequence of belief in God. Belief and trust dance together, hand in hand.

Praying for oneself is properly called petition. Praying for others is properly called intercession, that is, prayer by a person between one in need and God with his benevolence. It is tempting to think of prayer as simply asking God for benefits to be conferred on others or on oneself, but prayer is more than making requests. It should start with worship, recognizing the worth of the glory of God, continue with admission of our own unworthiness-often so important, followed by an outburst of thanks for forgiveness and for all that God does for us, known or unknown. Then perhaps at last we are able to see our requests in context and receive the corresponding gifts of the Holy Spirit.

We so often ask for this or that without beginning to realize the implications. It may be in effect a request for a miracle, although it seems that God does not multiply miracles unnecessarily. There is, of course, an alternative to "Please, God, do this," namely, "Please, God, help me and others to do this." We are so often the feet and hands of God. Now we are closer to the heart of prayer—a seeking to be transformed into the likeness of God as seen in Jesus, our exemplar and helper. At this point it is needful and natural to listen for an answer, a guide to our thoughts, a deepening of our trust, a heartening of goodwill, and a blossoming of love for others. No answer is in a very real sense an answer in the context of prayer, worthy of thankfulness, a new aspect of trust, and a silent confirmation of belief.

If these are the products of prayer, they obviously become "evidence for Christian belief." These products are both a result of existing belief and a means of developing and strengthening beliefs. Notice the sequence, developing and strengthening. Some static, entrenched beliefs have their place, but without the possibility of change they become inert, a basis for undue pride, and blinkered judgments of oneself and others. It is dangerous to open one's mind—more may fall out than is taken in. Taking such risks is the way forward, but only if we have sufficient trust in God that all will be well. It is even possible that God will tell us to "taste and see," to think and act with honesty and imagination, and be prepared yet again to revise our beliefs, move farther forward, or even to retreat to previous positions. Above all we should avoid stagnation.

The relevance of "Evidence from Meditation and Prayer" now becomes clear. If prayer leads to changes of our belief, outside the presently accepted expressions of belief, it is not an easy path for us or for our family to follow, and may not be for a wider community, be it church or even a group within the dispersion of unbelievers. Seeking truth is very different from seeking comfort.

LEX ORANDI, LEX CREDENDI

This is sometimes translated as "the official prayers of the Church reveal the official beliefs of the Church," and this has certainly been the basis for the revision of the *Book of Common Prayer* (1662) along the way to *Common Worship* (2000). This rather overstates the "official" aspects, for the prayers of individuals also reveal their beliefs. It is worthwhile to meditate on alternative translations, such as:

> What rules prayer, rules belief.
> If you cannot pray it, you cannot believe it.
> What you pray is your ultimate basis for belief.

How do prayer and meditation influence our beliefs? By God acting with us, developing explicit and implicit beliefs, and clarifying and strengthening well-founded beliefs. The experience of prayer and meditation goes beyond "intellectual" beliefs and develops other qualities of faith, such as trust, awareness of providence, the need for repentance, and the joys of loving forgiveness.

In two books of intercessions and meditative prayers, listed in the bibliography, I have made well-founded scientific beliefs the basis for certain Christian beliefs and attitudes. For me, it is important to bring our developing beliefs into our conversation with God. That is equally true for changing our religious beliefs, sometimes arising from developing social perceptions. The role of women in the Church is being influenced by changes in society, and rightly so. One consequence is the dedication of our new thoughts by small but important changes in our prayers. For me, that puts the whole question of women priests and bishops just where it should be, on a person-to-person basis between the believer and God in prayer. Then each member of the Church, and leaders of the Church, can be well prepared to make a majority decision.

If, as I believe, the discoveries of science and evidence from the arts on one side and the revelation of God on the other are two sides of the same precious coin of experience of God's universe, then what more natural and proper than that both sides should together infuse, enliven, inspire, and add beauty and devotion to our prayers and meditations? Beliefs as the basis for prayer can lead to revisions of our beliefs. These revisions can then be reflected in our prayers and hopefully lead upward along an ascending spiral toward God, as revision by revision, we gradually approach nearer to the mind of God, however great the differences between creature and Creator.

Radiocarbon Dating

NUCLEI are composed of protons and neutrons, of closely similar masses. The number of protons, Z, known as the atomic number, determines the positive electric charge of the nucleus, and so the number of electrons in the atom, and hence its chemical properties. The number of neutrons, N, is known as the neutron number, and N plus the number of protons, Z, gives the atomic mass number, A. Isotopes are nuclei of the same chemical element with different masses, that is, different numbers of neutrons. The radioactive isotope Carbon-14 consists of six protons and eight neutrons and occurs in all living matter with a known very low abundance, one part in a million million parts of stable Carbon-12, $(Z = 6, N = 6)$, an abundance that is believed to have been approximately constant for many thousands of years. C-14 is formed from the Nitrogen-14 $(Z = 7, N = 7)$ in the atmosphere by collisions of cosmic ray particles. The reaction is in effect the replacement of a proton by a neutron. Carbon-14 decays by beta particle emission to stable Nitrogen-14 and for a given specimen, the age of which is to be determined, the "activity" is easily measured by the disintegrations per second. In *living* matter there are fifteen decays of Carbon-14 per second for every gram of Carbon-14, which contains 43,000 million million million C-14 nuclei. After the organic matter dies, the amount of Carbon-14 radioactivity decreases with a half-life, $t_{1/2}$, of 5,730 years, and measurements of the remaining activity enables ages of specimens to be deduced for ages up to about 50,000 years. There is an accurate check for woods up to several thousand years old afforded by the counting of the rings in a cross-section of the tree trunk. Agreement is impressive, but not exact.

The required formulae can be derived quite easily. The number of C-14 nuclei in a given carbon specimen is known from its measured mass to be n_0 at the time of its death. At the time of measurement of age, t years after its death, the number n_t is given by the well-known law of radioactivity $n_t = n_0 \exp(-\lambda t)$ (i.e., $n_t = n_0 e^{-\lambda t}$ or $n_0 = n_t e^{-\lambda t}$) where λ is the "radioactive constant."

A relation is needed between the age t, the measured ratio of activities n_t / n_0, and the known half-life $t_{1/2}$. First we relate λ to $t_{1/2}$. At the time $t_{1/2}$, by definition, n_t will be $n_0/2$, that is, $n_0/2 = n_0 \exp(-\lambda t_{1/2})$, and n_0 cancels.

Taking logs to the base e, $\log_e 1/2 = \_0.693 = -\lambda t_{1/2}$

or $\lambda = 0.693 / t_{1/2}$.

Substituting for λ in $n_0 / n_t = e^{-\lambda t}$, and taking logs to the base e,

$\log_e (n_0 / n_t) = \lambda t = (0.693/t_{1/2})t$

or $t_{1/2} = \log_e (n_0 / n_t) t_{1/2} / 0.693$

with $t_{1/2} = 5{,}730$ years, for C-14.

For an age t of 5,730 years,	$n_t = 0.50\, n_0$.
for t of 11,460 years,	$n_t = 0.25\, n_0$.
for t of 17,190 years,	$n_t = 0.125\, n_0$.
and for t of 2,865 years,	$n_t = 0.707\, n_0$.
for t of 1,432.5 years,	$n_t = 0.841\, n_0$.
for t of 573 years,	$n_t = 0.933\, n_0$.

Ages of Rocks

THE C-14 decay to N-14 is an example of decay to a stable daughter. For radiocarbon dating both the original activity of N-14 and the measured activity at the age of the specimen are known, and the formula derived above can be used.

Some rocks have no Strontium stable isotopes other than Strontium-87, but contain Rubidium-87, which undergoes β-decay with a half-life $t_{1/2} = 10^{10}$ years to stable Strontium-87. It is a reasonable assumption that when formed those rocks had no Strontium-87. The ratio of the abundances of stable daughter Sr-87 to parent Rb-87 allows the age of the rock to be determined. The required formula can be readily derived.

Let n_d be the number of stable daughter Sr-87 nuclei at the age t of the specimen. Let n_p be the number of parent nuclei Rb-87 at that same age. Let the radioactive constant of Rb-87 be λ.

As before $\quad n_p = n_p(\text{at } t = 0) \exp(-\lambda t)$

so $\qquad n_p(\text{at } t = 0) = n_p \exp(\lambda t)$

The number of daughter nuclei equals the number of parent decays,

$$n_d = n_p(\text{at } t = 0) - n_p$$

so $\qquad n_d = n_p \exp(\lambda t) - n_p = n_p(\exp(\lambda t) - 1)$

and the ratio daughter to parent $= n_d / n_p = \exp(\lambda t) - 1$,

or $\qquad n_d / n_p + 1 = \exp(\lambda t)$.

Taking logs to the base e,

$$\log_e (n_d / n_p + 1) = \lambda t = (0.693 / t_{1/2}) \, t$$

yielding $\quad \mathbf{t_{1/2}} = \log_e (\, n_d / n_p + 1) \, \mathbf{t}_{1/2} / 0.693.$

We can check this formula for an age of $t_{1/2}$ at which time $n_d = n_p$.

so $\qquad t = \log_e (1 + 1) \, t_{1/2} \,/\, 0.693$,

$\qquad\qquad$ that is, $t = t_{1/2}$

$\qquad\qquad$ since $\log_e 2 = 0.693$.

Another example of this method is given by Samarium-147, which decays by alpha particle emission, with a half-life of 106 thousand million years, to the stable daughter Neodymium-143. Both Samarium-147 and Neodymium-143 occur as trace elements in diamonds and yield ages for diamonds ranging from 2 million years to 3,200 million years.

Other rocks can be dated by the measurement of the abundance of Potassium-40, which decays to stable Argon-40 with a half-life of 1,250 million years. Measurements of the amount of the gas Argon-40 formed need to be corrected for any loss of gas. Any loss of Argon-40 would lead to a smaller estimated age.

Bibliography

Direct references to sources, and footnotes, have been avoided as far as possible as this is meant to be a book that can be read with ease by all interested people. All quotations from the Bible (NRSV) have been given references. Names of authorities have been kept as few as possible to escape the tendency in some writings to suggest that mention of the opinion of a well-known name is sufficient to decide an issue.

Baker, J. A. *The Faith of a Christian.* London: Darton, Longman and Todd, 1996.

Barbour, I. G. *Religion in an Age of Science.* San Francisco: HarperSanFrancisco, 1990.

————. *Ethics in an Age of Technology.* New York: HarperCollins, 1992.

Burge, Ted. *Lord for All Seasons.* London: Canterbury Press, 1998.

————. *Lord of All, Hear Our Prayer: Intercessions and Meditations for Public Worship and Private Prayer.* 2d ed. London: Canterbury Press, 1999.

Butchins, Adair. *The Numinous Legacy: Modern Cosmology and Religion.* Aldershot, Hants: Albatross Press, 2002.

Coles, Peter, ed. *The Icon Critical Dictionary of the New Cosmology.* Cambridge, UK: Icon Books Ltd., 1998.

Dancy, John. *The Divine Drama: The Old Testament as Literature.* Cambridge, UK: Lutterworth Press, 2001.

Darwin, Charles. *The Illustrated Origin of Species.* Abridged and Introduced by Richard E Leakey. New York: Farrar, Straus, and Giroux, 1979.

Davies, Paul. *The Mind of God: The Scientific Basis for a Rational World.* New York: Simon and Schuster, 1992.

Gamow, George, and Russell Stannard. *The New World of Mr. Tompkins.* Cambridge: Cambridge University Press, 1999.

Goodwin, Simon, and John Gribbin. *Deep Space*. London: Constable, 1999.

Grant, R. M., with D. N. Freedman. *The Secret Sayings of Jesus (Gospel of Thomas)*. London: Fontana, 1960.

Greene, Brian. *The Elegant Universe: Superstrings, Hidden Dimensions, and the Quest for the Ultimate Theory*. New York: W. W. Norton and Company, 1999.

Gribbin, John. *Science: A History, 1543-2001*. London: Book Club Associates, 2002.

Gunton, E.C., S. R. Holmes, and M. A. Rae. *The Practice of Theology: A Reader*. London: SCM Press, 2001.

Habgood, J. *Faith and Uncertainty*. London: Darton, Longman and Todd, 1997.

Hawking, Stephen. *A Brief History of Time: From the Big Bang to Black Holes*. New York: Bantam, 1988.

————. *The Universe in a Nutshell*. New York: Bantam, 2001.

Hick, J., ed. *The Myth of God Incarnate*. Louisville, KY: Westminster John Knox Press, 1978.

Isserlin, B. S. J. *The Israelites*. London: Thames and Hudson, 2001.

James, Peter, Nikos Kokkinos, Robert Morkot, John Frankish, I. J. Thorpe, and Colin Renfrew. *Centuries of Darkness: A Challenge to the Conventional Chronology of Old World Archaeology*. London: Pimlico, 1991.

Mayne, Michael. *This Sunrise of Wonder: Letters for the Journey*. London: Fount, 1995.

————. *Learning to Dance*. London: Darton, Longman and Todd, 2001.

McCrum, Michael. *The Man Jesus: Fact and Legend*. London: Janus, 1999.

McGrath, A.E. *Christian Theology: An Introduction*. Oxford: Blackwell, 1994.

————. *Science and Religion: An Introduction*. Oxford: Blackwell, 1999.

The Doctrine Commission of the Church of England. *The Mystery of Salvation: The Story of God's Gift*. London: Church House Publishing, 1995.

Peacocke, Arthur. *From DNA to Dean: Reflections and Explorations of a Priest-Scientist*. London: Canterbury Press, 1996.

————. *Paths from Science Towards God.* Oxford: Oneworld, 2001.

Phillips, Graham. *The Moses Legacy: The Evidence of History.* London: Sidgwick and Jackson, 2002.

Polkinghorne, John. *Science and Creation: The Search for Understanding.* London: SPCK, 1988.

————. *Science and Christian Belief: Theological Reflections of a Bottom-up Thinker.* London: SPCK, 1994.

————. *Scientists as Theologians.* London: SPCK, 1996.

Redford, D. B. *Egypt, Canaan, and Israel in Ancient Times.* Princeton, NJ: Princeton University Press, 1992.

Ridsdale, L. *Evidence-Based General Practice.* Saunders, London: Bailliere Tindall, 1995.

Rohl, David. *The Lost Testament.* London: Century, 2002.

Ross, H. M. *Jesus Untouched by the Church: His Teachings in the Gospel of Thomas.* London: Sessions, 1998.

Staniforth, Maxwell, and Andrew Louth. *Early Christian Writings: The Apostolic Fathers.* Penguin Classics. London: Penguin Books, 1987.

Stannard, Russell. *Science and Wonders: Conversations about Science and Belief.* London: Faber and Faber, 1996.

————. *The God Experiment.* London: Faber and Faber, 1999.

————, ed. *God for the Twenty-first Century.* Philadelphia: Templeton Foundation Press, and London: SPCK, 2000.

Stenger, Victor J. *Has Science Found God? The Latest Results in the Search for Purpose in the Universe.* New York: Prometheus Books, 2003.

Sturgis, Matthew. *It Ain't Necessarily So.* London: Headline, 2001.

Zimmer, Carl. *Evolution: The Triumph of an Idea.* London: William Heinemann, 2001.

Index